THE MAKING OF LEEDS

THE MAKING OF Series

'The Making of' series is a new and fascinating collection, brought to you by Wharncliffe Books. The series is not intended to be a chronological account of an area, but to highlight the prominent factors which bring to life the development and 'character' of each town. These highly illustrated books contain illuminating snapshots captivating the history and nostalgia of each locality.

Other titles in the series

The Making of Manchester, Mike Fletcher
ISBN 1-903425-32-8
£9.99

The Making of Huddersfield, George Redmonds
ISBN 1-903425-39-5
£9.99

The Making of Sheffield, Melvyn Jones
ISBN 1-903425-42-5
£9.99

The Making of the South Yorkshire Landscape, Melvyn Jones
ISBN 1-871647-75-4
£9.95

The Making of the West Yorkshire Landscape, Anthony Silson
ISBN 1-903425-31-X
£9.99

The Making of Liverpool, Mike Fletcher
ISBN 1-903425-53-0
£9.99

Other titles of interest

Leeds Pals, Laurie Milner
ISBN 0-85052-335-4
£17.95

Aspects of Leeds 2, Lynne Stevenson-Tate
ISBN 1-871647-59-2
£9.95

Aspects of Leeds 3, Lynne Stevenson-Tate
ISBN 1-903425-05-0
£9.99

Foul Deeds and Suspicious Deaths in Leeds, David Goodman
ISBN 1-903425-08-5
£9.99

Please contact us via any of the methods below for more information or a catalogue.
WHARNCLIFFE BOOKS
47 Church Street – Barnsley – South Yorkshire – S70 2AS
Tel: 01226 734555 – 734222 Fax: 01226 724438
E-mail enquiries@pen-and-sword.co.uk – Website: www.wharncliffebooks.co.uk

The Making of
LEEDS

David Goodman

Series Editor
Brian Elliott

Wharncliffe Books

First Published in Great Britain in 2004 by
Wharncliffe Local History
an imprint of
Pen and Sword Books Ltd.
47 Church Street
Barnsley
South Yorkshire
S70 2AS

ISBN: 1-903425-41-7

A CIP catalogue record for this book is available from the
British Library.

Typeset in 10/12pt Plantin by Mac Style Ltd, Scarborough.

Printed and bound in England by
CPI UK.

Pen and Sword Books Ltd incorporates the Imprints of
Pen & Sword Aviation, Pen & Sword Maritime,
Pen & Sword Military, Wharncliffe Local History,
Pen & Sword Select, Pen and Sword Military Classica
and Leo Cooper.

For a complete list of Pen & Sword titles please contact
PEN & SWORD BOOKS LIMITED
47 Church Street
Barnsley
South Yorkshire
S70 2BR
England
E-mail: enquiries@pen-and-sword.co.uk
Website: www.pen-and-sword.co.uk

Contents

Front cover: *The Packhorse Inn*, Leeds. David Goodman collection
Back cover: (Upper) *Kirkgate Market*. David Goodman collection
            (Lower) *Kirkstall Abbey*. David Goodman collection

$\mathcal{I}$NTRODUCTION

I was a little surprised when asked by Wharncliffe to write *The Making of Leeds*. Though I have lived in Leeds for about fourteen years, I wasn't born there and don't feel that the city has shaped me in the way that Hull, the city of my birth has. So, I cannot claim to be a fully fledged Loiner, unlike several others who have their names in print with books relating to Leeds. However, I have no hesitation in saying that I have enjoyed this project and have learnt much about the city in the process. Now the finished product is before you, I hope and believe it to be a worthy addition to the bookshelves.

I have to confess to knowing little about the city's rich and varied history before studying it. Moreover, though I have obviously travelled through the city centre on foot on many occasions, I have walked through without paying any attention to what is around me. That is a shame as I was soon to realise that when I took the trouble to look at the architecture and the environment around me, there were some beautiful buildings, which are passed by hundreds, perhaps thousands of people every day of the week. However, only a tiny proportion of those people would know anything about the rich history of those buildings and the fascinating stories they could tell.

For instance, I enjoyed researching the chapter on education and when writing about the formation of the Leeds School Board in 1870 I realised that I passed its original building almost every day of the week!

Many of the buildings in Leeds city centre have historical significance and the Leeds Civic Trust deserve great credit for its Blue Plaques Scheme which has given greater prominence to the buildings in question as well as providing something of an insight into the reasons why a particular building is of such historical importance. The scheme gave me a starting point when it came to looking at the part of Leeds' history which is still around us.

There are several books which perhaps aim to be regarded as a fully comprehensive account of the history of this great city. *The Making of Leeds* could never claim to be that as it would need a book several times this size to even begin to undertake such a task. However, what this book can do is give a glimpse into Leeds' past and a look at how the city has evolved in some crucial areas.

There are already books on Leeds which concentrate on the history of the woollen industry, the history of religion or transport. However this book, ambitiously tries to look at twelve key areas in the development of the city and give perhaps a briefer insight into how Leeds came to be the place we know today. Much of the material for the book has come from local papers of the time and this is why there is perhaps more information on Victorian Leeds than other eras.

It is fascinating to think of Leeds in times past, and it is a credit to those in authority, that much of it has been maintained, giving those of us with an interest in local history, at least some idea of how Leeds has developed and changed through the years.

As usual there are many people to thank during the making of *The Making of*. Brian Elliott and the rest of the staff at Wharncliffe have always been happy to discuss all aspects of the book. Also helpful have been the staff at Leeds Central Library, especially those in the Local Studies department, who have had a regular visitor these last few months. I'll be there a little less often from now but I fully appreciate the hard work undertaken by the staff.

My friends at the Thoresby Society deserve special praise. On my irregular visits to their home I have been made a very welcome guest and they have been full of helpful advice, especially regarding photographs.

Finally, thank you to my family. Our now annual New Year's Day outing to take photographs was postponed due to snow, much to their disgust. However, I was able to restore the smile to their faces when we went out on a freezing cold Sunday morning in February.

1   *P*OPULATION

eeds has been in existence for over 1,000 years in one shape or another. It was on or near the site of an old Roman encampment and was a fortified town in the days of the Venerable Bede who made mention of the settlement in AD 731. Its strength made it a natural target for attack during the Norman Conquest and thereafter, for several generations the Pagenals were its feudal lords after Albert de Lacy granted most of the Manor of Leeds to Ralph Paganel.

In Roman times it is accepted that Leeds must have been in a position of some importance as it was situated upon and was uniting so many of the Roman roads. Further evidence of the importance of the settlement can be gleaned by the fact that Leeds also once had a castle. It originally stood on Mill Hill near Bishopgate Street and was thought to have been built by Ilbert de Lacy, who was also responsible for the building of Pontefract Castle.

At the time that the castle was in existence, Leeds was a mere agricultural village, though it also had a tower at Lydgate near to where St John's Church now stands.

East Bar. The stone marked the eastern boundary of the medieval town of Leeds. The author

Despite its position at the centre of many Roman roads, for some centuries Leeds was quite small, steadily advancing as a market for wool and sheepskin though inferior to some other Yorkshire and Lincolnshire market towns. At this time there were few signs of prosperity, but as Lancashire and Yorkshire became great centres of manufacturing, Leeds quickly established itself as the main town on the eastern side of the Pennines. The town benefited from having Hull as its nearest major port in much the same way as Manchester became reliant on Liverpool.

In Tudor times, Leeds was still concentrated around very few streets including Vicar Lane, Albion Street and Boar Lane. It had a market and a parish church, but little else and was surrounded on all sides by thick woodland. Its boundaries had only just reached out to the areas now known as Woodhouse, Burley and Holbeck.

The population of Leeds increased to around 3,000 towards the end of the sixteenth century and by 1626 it was of sufficient size to have Sir John Saville appointed as the first Mayor or Alderman. His coat of arms comprised the now famous hanging sheep and was intended to indicate the town's prominence as a centre for the manufacturing of wool.

During the seventeenth century Leeds became the main town in the country for selling cloth and as people were attracted to the town

The Scarborough Hotel, *former site of the Leeds Manor House.* The author

due to work, more public houses, shops and merchant houses were built.

At around this time the travel writer Celia Fiennes described the town, saying:

Leeds is a large town, several large streets, clean and well paved and good houses, all built of stone, some have good gardens and steps up to their houses and walls before them. This is esteemed the wealthiest town of its size in the county.

Most buildings during the 1500s and 1600s had been made of oak-framed wattle, daub walls and thatched roof, though some were built of stone as there were many stone quarries in the area. Only a few of the richer inhabitants had houses that were larger and more ostentatious. In 1628 Red Hall, built near the junction of the Headrow and Albion Street, was reputably the first house in Leeds to be built in brick.

In 1600 the population of Leeds was about 3,000, and it doubled in the hundred years to 1700 despite the Civil War and the plague having accounted for many people. The central township was increasingly populated and new houses were being built in the open spaces bordering the main streets. By the early years of the eighteenth century Leeds was still based on its basic medieval pattern centered around the main streets of Briggate, Kirkgate, Boar Lane, Vicar Lane and the upper and lower Headrow.

Between 1700 and 1771 the town continued to grow at a remarkable pace and the population rose from about 6,000 to over 16,000. Still, however, the boundaries of Leeds had not extended out at a pace in keeping with the rise in numbers, meaning increased pressure for space within the town. So most of the extra people who had come into the town were housed within that medieval boundary in buildings constructed within existing yards and gardens.

The expanding population was largely down to the growth of wool and cloth production in the area. People were drawn to Leeds as it became regarded as the main market town in the West Riding. The city was blessed with low rents and easy access to facilities for woollen production. There were also, despite the overcrowding, small plots of land available for people wishing to keep livestock.

In 1772 a massive housebuilding project began with over 3,000 houses built within the Leeds township. Within twenty years that number had been doubled and the number of houses built in Leeds grew at a rate of about five per cent a year with almost every available piece of land being built on.

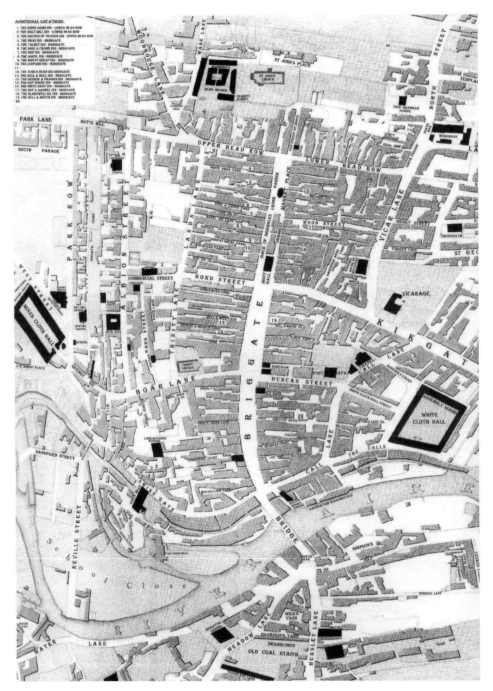

Harrison's map of Leeds. Showing many of the Leeds landmarks of the time including White Cloth Hall and the Mixed Cloth Hall. Author's collection

The 1780s saw the building of the first two-story 'back to back' terraced streets to house the growing labour force. Largely built in York Street and the Quarry Hill area, over the next 150 years, thousands of 'back to backs' were built up all over Leeds, providing accommodation for the large numbers of people coming to the town to work in the mills and engineering works.

The better off began to flee from the overcrowding and moved up to the villages and the surrounding countryside. By 1790 the population had grown to about 25,000, a four-fold increase since 1700 and Leeds had become one of the ten biggest towns in the country.

The first census in 1801 put the population of Leeds at just over 30,000 making it the fifth largest town, surpassed by Bristol, Birmingham, Liverpool and Manchester.

Between the opening of the Town Hall in Leeds by Queen Victoria in 1858 and the First World War in 1914, Leeds continued to expand with a large amount of mass inward migration of people from elsewhere in Yorkshire and other parts of England.

The rise in the population during this period of time arose from a situation where the number of births exceeded the death rate as well as the net in-migration of people coming into Leeds from other parts of the United Kingdom and towards the end of this period, from Eastern Europe. In-migration into Leeds accounted for about a third of the increase in population which Leeds experienced in the nineteenth century.

Two groups of immigrants were especially significant as the century progressed. The Irish settled in Leeds in increasingly large numbers from the early years of the nineteenth century and by 1841 there were 5,000 Irish settlers in the area, some six per cent of the population.

The effects of the potato famine in Ireland caused many to flee to England from across the Irish Sea and the Irish community, which had reached 10,000 by 1851 peaked at about 15,000 in 1861, which at the time was about an eighth of the total population. Largely congregated mainly in the Kirkgate and Bank districts of the city, it was the largest Irish community in Yorkshire.

The settlers did not always meet the approval of the indigenous population as the Reverend Edward Jackson described them in June 1847:

Tall men with long coats and hats without crowns, and women, wild and haggard, with numbers of unearthly looking children – strange beings that run alongside of the men and women, and looked at you out of the corner of their eyes, with a sort of half-frightened half-savage expression. The usual low lodging houses for this class of people were soon more than full and they extemporised for themselves dwellings such as none but they would have occupied.

Why the poor law authorities did not bestir themselves in time and open proper places for the reception of these wretched exiles, seems now a strange blunder. Being Irish I suppose they were not legally chargeable to township. But it was a great mistake and a woeful economy; that the emigrants brought with them not only hunger, but death. In a very short time the frightful Irish fever [typhus] was epidemic in all the lower parts of the town.

In the 1880s a new wave of immigrants, this time Jews escaping the pogroms of Eastern Europe, arrived in the town. Most of these newcomers settled down to work in the ready-made clothing industry.

The Jewish community dated back to the eighteenth century when it was estimated that there were about 500 Jewish families living in Leeds in 1877. The community grew thereafter from an estimated 6,000 in 1888, to 15,000 in 1902 and to over 20,000 by 1911, making it the biggest centre of Jewish population outside London.

The vast majority lived in the Leylands area and around Camp Road where the streets were about eighty-five per cent Jewish. They congregated together and their religion, orthodox dress and distinctive Yiddish language occasionally gave rise to anti-Semitism. As with the Irish immigrants before them, they were branded as 'dirty people' and their reputation was not aided by tales of long hours and grim conditions in their tailoring sweatshops, which were sprouting up, also predominantly in the Leylands area.

Victorian England saw rapid change within the country. It was becoming the 'workshop of the world' and the growth in industrialisation as well as urbanisation was a trend that Leeds was closely associated with.

However, the industrial success came at a price. The smoky atmosphere of the town during the Industrial Revolution was responsible for killing many trees in the centre of Leeds and many statues became covered in soot. For all the positive changes which came about due to the growth in industry, as one commentator of the time said 'Smoke and Leeds are almost as inseparably connected in the public mind as bacon and eggs.'

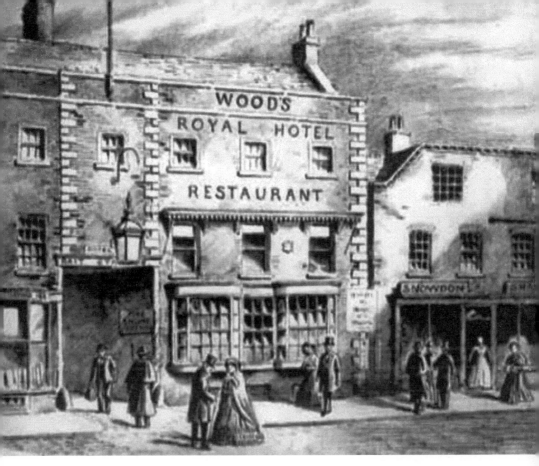

Briggate in 1870. Thoresby Society

In 1849 journalist Angus Reach travelled throughout Britain and reported on the state of some of the major cities. He included Leeds in his travels and did not appear to be too impressed. He wrote:

Leeds has little or none of that hothouse appearance which to some extent distinguishes Manchester. It seems in its physical peculiarities a more substantial and slower growing town than its high-pressure cotton neighbour, and it possesses none of the metropolitan attributes of the latter. Leeds has no public parks. With here and there an exceptional spot, the suburbs extend in mean, clumsy, straggling streets out into the bare country.

There are no such fair ranges of villas as those which in many quarters skirt the busy portions of Manchester: and the dwellings of the labouring class, to which I shall speedily call attention, are, in point of appearance, and of symmetrical outward an convenient inward arrangement, decidedly inferior to those of the cotton capital ...

The historic courtyard of Queens Court. The author

Urbanisation developed because home and work were physically tied together. Hours of work were long; there was no public transport and walking was often the only means of getting about. Many workers only had casual jobs so had to live very near the places where work was widely available, resulting in the industrial townships also becoming the main residential areas.

However, by 1851, transport had improved, especially with the advent of the railways and Leeds was becoming socially segregated with the middle classes setting up residence on the outer edges of Leeds leaving the working classes to remain in the industrialised inner city.

The population grew to 88,000 in 1841. Meanwhile, the town's workforce, including women and children, also grew from about 12,000 in 1790 to over 35,000 in 1841.

Park Square was a high class residential area, being home to merchants, lawyers and surgeons. The author

In 1911 the census gave the population of Leeds as 450,000. In this respect Leeds reflected a thriving modern town but in reality, industrialisation and urbanisation led to increasing overcrowding and squalor.

Poverty

The incomes of working class families were just enough to keep themselves intact. However, they were unable to amass any savings so that when faced with illness, old age or unemployment, they were simply unable to cope. For many in this position, parish poor relief was their only salvation. Most of the poor were given some money from the poor rates and were able to remain in their homes, but those with other disadvantages, mainly the aged, the sick or the very young were placed in the workhouse.

The seventeenth century workhouse in Lady Lane closed in 1705, but reopened about twenty years later with the purpose of 'more orderly and easily regulating and relieving the poor of the township.' Many in the workhouse were already ill when they arrived and disease quickly spread through those with the misfortune of staying there. In January 1741 a quarter of its inmates died due to a smallpox epidemic.

The workhouse was a permanent fixture in Leeds throughout the centuries and the stigma attached to being forced to accept charity reduced. During the first few years of the twentieth century older people had to be literally forced to go and live in the workhouse in order to escape starvation. However, once they were in they showed less reluctance to re-enter again if they, once again, were forced into hard times.

Slowly there came to be less prejudice against people who lived in the poorhouse and it led to plans in 1906 to almost double its size as the early years of the twentieth century had seen a rise of about 700 in the number of people who were designated as paupers.

Royal seal of approval

During the 1850s Leeds was at its height in terms of its growth and its birth as a town of real importance was confirmed when it was announced that Queen Victoria would come to Leeds to open the Town Hall in 1858.

Thousands were on the streets on their arrival in the town and the Great Northern Railway had special platforms with galleries erected. The following day all the Sunday scholars and teachers in the borough, about 30,000, were massed together on platforms on Woodhouse Moor where special hymns and anthems were sung. There was a passage between the two galleries where the Queen, Prince Albert and the accompanying royal party passed between them.

There was also a mass of people, approximately 70,000, on the banks of the reservoir and when the Queen appeared on the Moor the children struck up the national anthem.

Israel Roberts, in his autobiography of Leeds, remembered the day when the Queen came to town:

The street decorations on the whole line of the route were magnificent and many of the shopkeepers on Briggate had most elaborate and expensive devices in front of their premises. Appleby, the cheesemonger had the whole of his shop covered with dahlias to the number of 30,000. Over the dahlias there hung a grand silk flag inscribed with the words, 'peace on earth and goodwill to all men'.

Just before the Queen passed the shop, the proprietor had the street strewn with flowers which soldiers guarded until the Queen's carriage had driven over them.

During the Great Exhibition of 1851 trips were run to London from Leeds for half a crown return and a trip to London for the same price was arranged for the day in 1858 when the Queen and Prince Albert came to Leeds as it was thought that the offer would take some people out of town to ease congestion.

Much of today's Leeds is of Victorian origin with many impressive and imposing buildings built at this time. Many of these buildings were designed by the Victorian architect from Hull called Cuthbert Broderick. His buildings include the Town Hall, the Leeds Mechanics' Institute, the Civic Theatre and the famous domed Corn Exchange of 1861. The dome in the corn exchange allowed sunlight in so that merchants could clearly see the quality of the grain they were buying.

Leeds is well known for its shopping arcades off the main shopping streets of Headrow and Briggate. These date mainly from the late Victorian period and include Thornton's Arcade and the County Arcade. Thornton's Arcade was the first of the arcades and was opened in 1877 by Charles Thornton, a Music Hall owner. The arcade is best known for its clock which features animated characters from Sir Walter Scott's *Ivanhoe*. Robin Hood and Gurth the Swineherd strike the quarter hours, Friar Tuck and Richard the Lionheart strike the hours.

Leeds Civic Hall. The author

The Dysons clock was a meeting place for many Leeds residents. The author

2 ℛELIGION

Early religion

At the time of the Domesday Book, Leeds was a small village numbering only about 200 people who settled near a crossing on the River Aire. Paulinus, priest of Leeds, was the first accredited vicar and almost certainly lived during the twelfth century as he is stated to have been a witness at a miracle performed on Whit Sunday 1177, by St William of York in restoring sight to a blind Leeds girl.

Kirkstall Abbey. The author

The only surviving example of Norman architecture in Leeds is the church in Adel which dates back to 1150 though the first church to be built in Leeds itself is likely to have been on the site of the Leeds Parish Church, some time in the seventh century. A church in the area was mentioned in the Domesday Book and was extended during Norman times. Probably built in wood, it is thought to have been burnt by King Penda of Mercia in 633 and was eventually rebuilt in stone. Proof of Saxon churches can be found by the presence of fragments of six crosses which survived from that time. There is also the reconstructed free-standing cross in St Peter's Church.

Kirkstall Abbey was a significant building in the expansion of Leeds. The Cistercian monks were farmers, who cleared and drained the land which was unsuitable for arable production, but perfect for sheep farming. The demand for this type of wool grew and Italian and French merchants bought it in bulk. A small wharf existed near Kirkstall Abbey from where barges transported this wool along the Aire and then the Humber to Hull from where it was transported abroad.

Organised religion took a step forward in the early part of the seventeenth century when, after a dispute over the appointment of a Vicar of Leeds, a body was set up to ensure that in the future, appointments would have to be ratified by the laity. Church bodies were also in dispute with senior Leeds citizens on the issue of local charities. A solution came in the form of a special committee, founded primarily by the citizens of Leeds to distribute charity money.

Leeds developed a Puritan tradition during the seventeenth century and appointed Robert Cooke as the towns first Puritan vicar, the first of several in Leeds during this time. By the time Cooke died in 1615, the parish was in a state of quandary. Though there were six chapels serving the out-townships of the parish, the parish church itself was too small for the growing congregation.

The 1628 survey of the manor referred to the overcrowding, saying:

The Church of Leeds (which is a verie faire church built after a cathedrall structure and having one side thereof double Iled) is soe besett with scaffold over scaffold [wooden galleries] *soe as noe place is voide to heare ye Minister.*

A new church, St John's, was the solution, and with the help of the benefactor John Harrison, the patron of Leeds Grammar School, it was built in Upper Briggate in 1631; the tomb of Harrison exists inside the church.

St John's Church. The author

As the population of Leeds continued to grow, several new churches and chapels were built and existing buildings tried to expand in order to increase their seating capacity. Religious persecutions at the beginning of the reign of Charles II led to the issuing of the Declaration of Indulgence, an act that allowed all religious sects to worship as they wished. The declaration led to the building of the first Mill Hill Chapel in 1672 as the first Nonconformist meeting house in Leeds.

Trinity Church was the third church to be established in Leeds. Built in Boar Lane in 1727, it was initially intended to be for the use of the local gentry and rich merchants.

The Victorian times brought a religious revival which transformed the area and encouraged many of the population to embrace religion once more. Dr Walter Hook was invited to become Vicar of Leeds in

Mill Hill Chapel. The author

1837 despite having a reputation as a 'high churchman' whilst Leeds was known as a stronghold of Dissenters. During his time in Leeds the town, through its role in the cloth trade, was at the forefront of the industrial revolution sweeping Britain and leading to a population explosion in the area.

By 1840 the population of the borough of Leeds had leapt to over 150,000 and even a man as hardworking as Dr Hook was struggling to keep control of its religious affairs. As a result he sought to give the ancient chapelries the right to administer their own affairs and promoted the Leeds Vicarage Act which received Royal Assent on 9 August 1844.

This Act divided Leeds into twenty-one parishes, resulting in each parish receiving fees for baptisms, weddings and funerals whereas previously the fees had been payable to the Vicar of Leeds.

Dr Hook was also passionately interested in education of the young, especially those from poorer backgrounds. He wanted to see all children receive at least a basic form of education and saw it as a duty of the church to ensure this happened. His informal campaign came at the same time as parliament was seeking to introduce the 'Ten Hour Bill' to reduce the number of hours children could work in mills and factories. As some of the factory and mill owners attended the Parish Church, Dr Hook did not flinch from reminding them, from the pulpit, of their duties to help those who could not help themselves.

Hook's achievements in Leeds can be reflected in statistics. When he came to Leeds there were only eight churches in the town and nine in the suburbs. He raised the number to thirty-six and saw the number of parsonage houses rise from six to thirty-nine and schools from three to thirty. He also strayed from his

Dr Walter Farquhar Hook engraved by C E Wagstaff from Rosenburg's portrait, 1835. Thoresby Society

religious duties to keep an eye on the general welfare of the town of Leeds. It was Dr Hook who urged the town council to purchase Woodhouse Moor and convert it into a public park.

A religious magazine of the early 1900s looked back on Hook's time in Leeds and praised his contribution to its religious welfare:

What a contrast between the Leeds that Dr Hook entered in 1837 and the one he left in 1859. He found it a stronghold of dissent, he left it a stronghold of the church. He found it one parish, he left it many parishes. That is a magnificent tribute to Hook's massive churchmanship and practical energy and the work that he did for the church in Leeds maybe regarded as a firmly held heritage which still gives to the Vicar of Leeds the well founded position of an acknowledged centre of social and philanthropic movements and of that which makes for what is best in the life of the city.

Leeds Parish Church, as it has stood since 1858. The author

When Hook was installed as vicar in 1837, the town's religious leaders were already decided in their view that the Parish Church did not fit the requirements of the expanding and vibrant town which Leeds had become.

Therefore the old medieval Parish Church was demolished and rebuilt in 1841 at a cost of nearly £30,000. The tower in the new church contained thirteen bells and was darker inside largely due to a greater amount of stained glass. There was seating accommodation for about 3,000. The church was also equipped with a modern organ:

For such a function, Leeds Parish Church, magnificent as a cathedral, with its rich carvings of old oak and its wealth of stained glass and with the brilliant sunshine illuminating the beautiful windows and enveloping the crowded scene in an atmosphere of soft coloured light, the picture was an inspiring and deeply impressive one.

The new building revitalised the role of the church in religious Leeds and through the years it enjoyed a reputation for the high prestige and high character of its vicars, it was also commonplace for the church to act as a nursery for English bishops. The church was a place of worship fit for the town and for a time it reverberated to the gentle tones of Dr Hook's sermons. However, after over twenty years in Leeds the vicar was offered the Deanery of Chichester and so, on Wednesday, 29 June 1859 he preached his last sermon as Vicar of Leeds.

As one example of his good nature and acceptance of all the people in Leeds, when Dr Hook first came to the town the Stop the Charter spirit was in full cry and some agitators attended a church meeting in full force and put in twelve chartists as church wardens, which they could legally do. However, Dr Hook accepted them in good part and subsequently said he had never had twelve more efficient men. On the following Sunday the church was crowded with chartists who claimed the right to occupy all the private seats.

Memorial to Dr Walter Hook, situated in Leeds Parish Church. Thoresby Society

Catholicism

The increase in population brought about by the industrial revolution, together with the Irish immigration of the 1840s onwards meant that urban areas continued to grow whilst rural areas declined and the Catholic community was no different in moving towards the city by the 1860s.

During the latter part of the eighteenth century, when Leeds had a population of about 30,000 there were only approximately ten Catholic families living in the town, meaning the total population of Catholics in Leeds was less than fifty. Until 1786, in order to attend Mass the people had to travel out of the city by whatever method they could, often by foot, to Roundhay or Stourton, as these were the only places which had a priest and a small chapel.

Catholicism changed in Leeds around 1779 with the appointment of the Reverend Bernard Albert Underhill, of the Roundhay Mission. From the beginning of his time in Leeds he wanted to transfer the old established mission in Roundhay to Leeds to be more accessible to the people and in 1786 he managed to secure the use of a property in the centre of Leeds as a replacement. For this he was grateful for the intervention of Joseph Holdforth who was already a prominent member of the town's Catholic community.

Holdforth had obtained an agreement from the Vicar of Leeds and members of the Corporation for the establishment of a Roman Catholic place of worship and he also met the cost of hiring rooms to accommodate Underhill and a small chapel. This was on the second floor of a building next to the *Pack Horse Hotel* on the west side of Briggate.

Life for Underhill was far from easy as the records of the Dominican Order show:

> For a long time he had to struggle on in obscurity and poverty. His dwelling, with the room in which he assembled a few Catholics whom he could collect together to hear Mass, stood in a miserable alley or yard behind the public Shambles, and so straightened were his means that very often he had nothing more for dinner than potatoes mashed with buttermilk.

However, his devotion to duty was repaid in 1792 when he received a legacy of £600. He used the money to initiate the replacement of the upper room with a purpose-built chapel and a site was found at the junction of Lady Lane and Templar Lane. The foundation stone for the new chapel, called St Mary's, was laid in April 1793.

The *Leeds Guide* of 1806 described St Mary's as a beautiful building and it impressed those who came through its doors for worship. The focal point of the interior was the altar, above which hung a painting of the 'Descent from the Cross' by William Williams. St Mary's, as the only venue for Catholic worship in Leeds, became the focal point of the entire community which by now numbered several thousand, growing at the same rate as the city.

The community had been swollen by several thousand Irish Catholics who had arrived in Leeds by the 1820s and were mostly housed in overcrowded and insanitary conditions in the east end of the town. It was here that Father Oxley, who succeeded Father Underhill, renewed his efforts to expand the Leeds Mission. With financial help from some of the country's leading Roman Catholic families, he was able to open St Patrick's Chapel on York Road in July 1831, an occasion which was marked with a 'grand high mass and brilliant selection of vocal and instrumental music'.

At once the new church had a congregation numbering about four thousand. A memorial to Father Underhill was installed at St Patrick's and moved, with the church, to a new site in 1891. It stood as a reminder of the man, who for almost thirty years was 'the pastor of the congregation of Leeds'.

Diocese of Leeds

Before the nineteenth century the Diocese of Beverley covered the whole of Yorkshire with Dr John Briggs, formerly the Vicar Apostolic of the Yorkshire District becoming the first Bishop of Beverley.

He served as Yorkshire's bishop for twenty-five years until his death in January 1861 when he was buried in the churchyard at Hazlewood between Leeds and Tadcaster. By the 1860s his successor Robert Cornthwaite had left York to take up residence in Leeds, at Springfield House in Little Woodhouse, now part of Leeds University.

Cornthwaite felt that his leadership of the Diocese would be more effective if he lived in the same area as most of the Yorkshire Catholics were residing. Although there was good railway access from Leeds to other parts of Yorkshire, the move took him further away from other important Yorkshire towns including Hull and Middlesbrough, so he came to believe that the answer lay in the sub-division of the oversized Diocese. To take account of the growth of the Catholic population in Yorkshire and the number of clergy and parishes under his control, Cornthwaite suggested that a split was inevitable and took his fight to Rome.

His patience was eventually rewarded when on 20 December 1878 the newly elected Pope Leo XIII decreed that the Diocese of Beverley be divided into the two Dioceses of Leeds and Middlesbrough, though the news travelled slowly and notice of the Pope's decision did not reach Leeds until the following February.

The West Riding and the city of York became the Diocese of Leeds, while the Middlesbrough Diocese consisted of the rest of Yorkshire. Cornthwaite was appointed as the first Roman Catholic Bishop of Leeds and St Anne's Church in Leeds became the Cathedral Church of the new Diocese.

Methodism and Non-conformism

Methodism began in Leeds in 1742 when William Shent and his wife were converted, possibly through the influence of a small community which had already been established in Armley. The first place for worship was in a house at Nether Mills, then at Spitalfields and ultimately at the house of a basket maker called Matthew Chippendale at Quarry Hill.

This house, near to St Peter's Chapel, was later to become the first Wesleyan Methodist Chapel in Leeds. After agreement had been reached to turn the house into a chapel the builders managed to ensure that Chippendale and his family remained there until the chapel, which came to be known as Gold Boggart House, was virtually completed, whereupon the old building was finally demolished.

John Wesley opened Gold Boggart House in 1751 and five years later a meeting house was built near the White Cloth Hall.

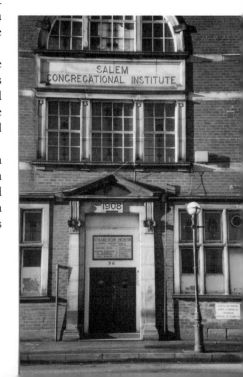

The new St Peter's superseded the old chapel in 1835 and thirteen years later this too was pulled down and part of the materials were used in the construction of the Richmond Hill chapel.

The eighteenth century was an uncertain time for Anglicans in Leeds as Methodism had established itself in the area and dissent was on the increase. Of concern to many was

Salem Congregational Church. The author

the increase in the number of people who came to be regarded as non-conformist.

This was also true of the nineteenth century and on Thursday, 19 December 1878, a large public meeting was held at the Albert Hall in Leeds under the auspices of the Leeds Non-Conformist Union. An organised opposition had been set up by a body of church defenders who were apparently under the impression that a resolution would be submitted in favour of disestablishment. The chairman, Mr J Barran MP spoke of the desirability of disestablishment and stated that a good many members of the Church of England thought that it to be undesirable to maintain the union between church and state.

Judaism

The first Jewish person thought to reside in Leeds was a man called Israel Benjamin of Vicar Lane whose burial was recorded in June 1739. It was said that he was born of the Jewish faith in Breslau, Germany though it is not recorded how he came to be in Leeds nor whether or not he was a practising Jew.

Leeds Jewry developed throughout the 1800s and had in its community many peddlers, mainly from those of Russian descent who had managed to make the arduous journey over from their homeland. The Russian pogroms did not begin effectively until 1881 but there was persecution of Jews in Russia from 1850 onwards, so many sought refuge in America and England.

Most set out from their homeland with the intention of crossing the Atlantic Ocean to seek a new life in America and, when they arrived in England, usually at the port of Hull, intended to travel across to Liverpool before catching the boat to the United States. However, as with many refugees who were intending to cross the Pennines and travel further west, many stopped and settled, some in Hull and many others in Leeds and Manchester.

Most of those who came at this time became peddlers, hawking their wares in Leeds and surrounding districts. They were usually without possessions when they joined others from Russia and collections were made within the community to provide them with enough for their first stocks of smallware or cheap jewellery.

However, by the 1850s and 1860s, there were many in the Jewish community who had become well-established in business in their adopted city as watchmakers, jewellers, pencil makers and chiropodists.

In 1851 Isaac Singer patented his first sewing machine and a non-Jewish tailor called John Barren was quick to see the benefit of it, applying it to the production of ready-made clothes. Another tailor, Herman Friend, had a small workshop in Templar Street and he began to make clothes to be sold in Barren's shop which was at the south end of Leeds Bridge. Friend devised the idea of a divisional labour system, a forerunner to the sweating system for which Leeds became notorious. Friend encouraged his employees to send for their relatives in Russia and Poland and as quickly as they arrived, Friend found them jobs in the tailoring trade.

As the community grew it was felt necessary to have a synagogue as there was a need for a focal point from where to say daily or weekly prayers. At the time the Leeds Jews were almost exclusively congregated around the Leylands district of the city. Belgrave Street was in this area and it was here that the first Leeds synagogue was built in 1860.

By this time there was already tension within the community which was in danger of being split. It was divided between those who had originated from the early settlers and those who derived from the immigrants who had more recently arrived.

There was also still suspicion amongst the indigenous people of Leeds to the Jews, perhaps demonstrated by a society in 1867 which promoted Christianity amongst the Jewish community. The society heard that there was still amongst the Jewish population in Leeds a 'remarkable readiness to receive the word of God'. A meeting for the society heard that during 1867 three Jews had been baptised in St George's Church. At the meeting a Reverend Maughan of Armley said that he could not understand the argument that the Jews were unlikely people to preach the Gospel. He said that he had lived amongst the Jews for some time and their outward circumstances were more respectable than many Christians. Their houses were 'exceedingly clean, their habits temperate and they were not susceptible to profane language'.

Leeds and religion

Religion in the nineteenth century was still important to many in the community. As Leeds grew so did the number of people coming into the town who wanted a place of worship, despite the growth of alternative attractions. The Leeds Church Extension, in existence since the mid-1850s, was set up as a reaction to a constantly increasing demand for additional church accommodation in all parts of the town.

As many in the population began to settle in other parts of Leeds, places of worship were seen in all parts of the town, leading to a fresh demand for those 'left behind' in the inner-city. In 1866 at Mount St Mary's, the new Roman Catholic Church opened and the Reverend Canon Cooke agreed that suitable churches already existed in other parts of Leeds, but that a church was needed in that part of Leeds because of the religious needs of the working classes, who had remained close to the centre of town.

On 29 October 1866 the first foundation stone was laid at the Leeds Church Institute in Albion Place. The Institute, founded by Dr Hook, was to be the permanent residence of the Church Institute and the Sunday School association.

Leeds Church Institute. The author

Many in Leeds warmly welcomed it with a newspaper report saying that every friend of the church must have:

> *long felt that the institute could never hope to assume that prominent position amongst the religious and educational institutions of the town, to which its high aims and unquestionable importance entitled it unless it possessed a building of its own.*

The paper added that the new building would be a means of showing the people of Leeds and beyond that the church 'was by no means a dormant institution but had awakened and shaken off its sloth.'

The Church Institute celebrated its golden jubilee in 1907 and the celebration gave the people of Leeds a reason to evaluate religion in the city. The papers in Leeds were fulsome in their praise of the Institute, which, during its existence, was the centre and focus of church life in the city. One said:

> *In a real sense the Institute has developed into the church house of Leeds, providing accommodation for many church organisations, acting as an information bureau on church matters and giving to all the parishes in the city a common centre and meeting place.*

The *Sunday Strand* added to the warm tributes to the organisation, commenting:

> *I suppose that there is not a town anywhere in England where the church and the non-conformists work together so much in harmony, as a general rule, as in Leeds. It said that the vicar of Leeds has always been able to rely on support from 'a large number of people who may not be of his own denomination, but who are always willing to assist in good work for the master.'*

Religion had a lasting effect on the daily and weekly life of many in Leeds in Victorian times. Sunday, as the day of rest, was observed to the full and no domestic work was undertaken except the essential. People cooked the dinner and made the bed but were not allowed to dust. The chips for loading the Monday morning fire had to be chopped on Saturday night and children were allowed to read only serious books and played no games.

Membership of churches and other places of worship peaked in the late Victorian and Edwardian eras. However, thereafter it declined and whereas a third of Leeds people regularly attended worship in

1900, this had dropped to about a sixth by the mid-1930s and to about an eighth by 1950.

As leisure options increased, they were more inviting for people who had previously been going to Sunday worship. The centenary brochure for Brunswick Chapel in 1925 tried to promote the benefits of religion, admitting:

The problems of today are very great for Brunswick. Through an ever-widening zone of Jews, four-fifths of our people come through miles of suburbs to worship in the old place ... One who lives on the outskirts of Leeds in the midst of sylvan quiet told the minister that on a certain Sunday last summer, after a day of brilliant sunshine as he sat in the cool of the early evening in his garden, he remarked to his wife, this has been a perfect day, I must close it fittingly, I want a service of great quiet, I am going down to Brunswick.

3 *T*RANSPORT

The River Aire is a main tributary in Yorkshire moving south-eastwards across the county before meeting up with the Humber and the North Sea. In prehistoric times it flowed through a wooded, swampy valley and it is here, at a ford over the river, that the village of Leeds was established.

Other villages such as Armley, Bramley, Headingley and Hunslet grew up on the rolling hills around it, however, it was Leeds, at that vital river crossing, which came to dominate the surrounding out-townships, gradually absorb them and ultimately dominate Yorkshire to become a major European city.

River transport was improved by the passing of the Aire and Calder Navigation Act in 1699 which allowed navigation along the two rivers to Goole and then onto Hull. This linked Leeds with its export markets for the first time and was a crucial factor in Leeds becoming a major exporter of woollen cloth in England.

The Aire and Calder Navigation in Leeds. Author's collection

The sheep on the Yorkshire moors provided the wool for the spinners and weavers working in Leeds and the surrounding villages. The position of Leeds as the main market for the trade in woollen goods was boosted in the eighteenth century by the building of the 127-mile long Leeds & Liverpool Canal which finally linked Leeds by canal with both of the major ports in the north; Liverpool in the west and Hull in the east.

The first section of the canal ran between Leeds and Gargrave. People and goods were carried down this canal, but as it was only the first section, goods were loaded and unloaded at Apperley Bridge where a new turnpike road crossed the canal.

The rapid rise of the railways through the 1800s did not immediately sound the death knell for river transport. Traffic on the Aire and Calder Navigation continued to rise with goods including coal, building stone, lime and salt continuing to travel by barge.

The Aire and Calder Navigation continued to run profitably, well into the twentieth century, only declining when the collieries of the Yorkshire region began to close down.

Leeds Bridge with the River Aire flowing through it. The author

The Rose & Crown Inn *was one of the famous Leeds coaching inns.* Thoresby Society

1873 saw the opening of the wrought and cast iron Leeds Bridge designed by Thomas Dyne Steele and built by John Butler Iron Works in Stanningley. This bridge replaced a several arched stone bridge, removed in 1869.

The Roman legacy, the road system, was supplemented during the Middle Ages by packhorse tracks linking the market centres and sometimes tracks were also laid to the site of navigable stretches of river. When the West Riding woollen trade began to expand in the sixteenth century, a new network of tracks were laid down, linking the upland areas of the Pennines with towns including Halifax, Wakefield and Leeds.

However, the roads in and around Leeds were in a terrible state up until the 1700s. They were almost impassable by single carts and

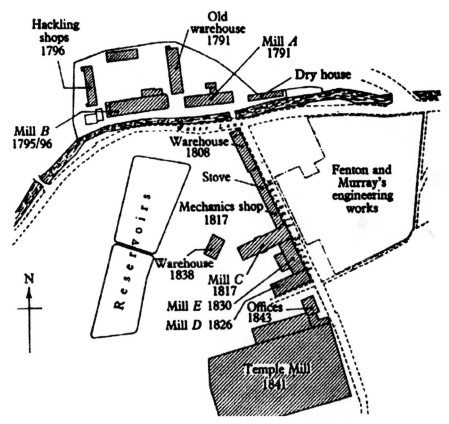

Diagram of John Marshall's Temple Mill and Matthew Murray's engineering works at Water Lane. The author

carriages of raw wool and manufactured goods were taken on the backs of single horses at a disadvantage of almost two hundred to one compared to travel by water.

In the 1700s, carriages were comparatively unknown, though the Sedan chair, which was introduced into Leeds in the 1600s, was still in evidence on the streets of the town, usually hired by ladies.

Long journeys on the primitive roads were not only hazardous due to the conditions, but also because of the chances of being hijacked by highwaymen. In common with the rest of the country, horses remained the main mode of transport for most with the animal being able to transport products, raw materials and people.

However, there was no incentive to keep roads in good condition until the seventeenth and eighteenth century when Parliament made

Matthew Murray. Thoresby Society

local turnpike trusts responsible for the construction and maintenance of specific lengths of road.

Leeds especially benefited from the Turnpike Act of the late eighteenth century which led to improvements in the route from Leeds to Selby; the natural outlet for merchandise which went through the port of Hull. Improvements were also made on the routes from Leeds to Elland, Bradford, Halifax and York. The moves were not universally popular as ratepayers objected to having to pay out for the cost of maintaining the roads whilst those actually using them were angry about the tolls they had to pay.

The situation deteriorated and there was mass resistance to paying with widescale rioting on the roads and in town. Armed gangs went on the rampage trying to burn the toll-houses and smash the gates, often meeting stiff resistance from the authorities.

In June 1753 what became known as the 'Leeds Fight' took place. A huge crowd of rioters went from Leeds with the intention of destroying the new turnpike at Harewood Bridge. However, Edwin Lascelles, the first Lord Harewood had been warned of this and gathered together about 300 of his tenants and workmen. It turned into a vicious fight between the two sides.

About a week later tempers became frayed once again when a man refused to pay a toll at Beeston turnpike and was arrested by soldiers brought in from York. Rioters demolished several bars and the *King's Arms* inn, as the meeting place of the magistrates and trustees of the turnpike, was right in the thick of the fray.

While three men were in the hands of the trustees at the hostelry, one evening a mob gathered in Lowerhead-row to rescue them. They broke the windows and the shutters of the *King's Arms* and tore up paving stones to throw at the soldiers. After failing to control the crowd by firing with a powder, the soldiers took to firing with bullets leaving the street strewn with wounded men, women and children.

Three people were killed and twenty-two wounded. As a result a military guard had to be set up over the *King's Arms* and at the houses of the Mayor and the Recorder.

The action taken, drastic as it was, led to the rioters retreating and the road improvement programme was able to proceed relatively unhindered. With the road improvements came new ways to travel and there was soon plenty of land travel on coaches between Yorkshire towns. Transport to other parts of the country also became possible and many of the inns down Briggate began to run coaches down to London. Before 1764 the journey to London was made 'god willing' in fourteen days. However, in that year the offer was made of 'safe and expeditious travelling with machines on steel springs in four days to London from *Ye Olde King's Arms* in Leeds every Monday and Wednesday'.

The time taken to reach London was reduced further to about two and a half days though some 'flying machines' made great virtue of the fact that they could do the journey in two days flat. This journey cost two guineas and a child carried on the lap was charged half-price.

By the end of the eighteenth century there were more adverts in the Leeds newspapers appearing and claiming 'cheap and expeditious travelling from Leeds to London' which would take passengers to London in two days stopping at Wakefield, Barnsley, Sheffield, Chesterfield, Mansfield, Nottingham, Leicester and Northampton. A typical journey involved setting out from the *Star and Garter* in Leeds every evening, arriving late afternoon in London. 'By which means the danger of travelling near the metropolis in the night will be entirely avoided.'

When travelling down to London there was always the risk of highwaymen stopping the coach, especially in the Highgate Hill area. Wagons also transported passengers to London from the *Golden Lion* in Briggate though these took five days to make the journey at a cost of five shillings. This way to travel also saw perils and pressgangs frequented main roads with many a wagon stopped and a pistol thrust into the driver's face.

The *Yorkshire Weekly News* reported on a trip from Leeds to York in 1813 made from the *Rose & Crown* in the Shambles. It gave an insight into the perils and the effort involved in a journey that would take about half an hour today:

The coach was the York Highflyer. It's timed to start at half past three, the horses are ready and the off-leader patiently paws the cobblestones;

the harness jingles and there is a ringing of glasses within the inn. The coachman climbs into his box and you and I take our places outside.

They aim to deliver copies of the Leeds Intelligencer into the city of York within three hours.

We clatter along ill-made streets, the man with the ribbons turning sharp corners with a simulated ease intended to convey to onlookers that he is immensely bored by the simplicity of it all. The guard unslings the long brass horn and gives a taste of his quality, a clarion challenge to the knights of the road. The horses were changed in Tadcaster.

By the beginning of the nineteenth century there were over forty coaches running in and out of Leeds daily and within fifteen years that number had doubled, making Leeds a major coaching centre.

Coaching remained throughout much of the early to mid-nineteenth century and even tried to survive the establishment of the railways. There were still coach proprietors trying to make their business survive in the face of ever stiff competition by changing routes or even combining services with the railways. However, the vast revenues had received a fatal blow and the railways gained a permanent footing in the nation's consciousness.

By the early nineteenth century Leeds was still a compact town, not big enough to support a passenger transport system. The suburbs didn't exist as the merchants and the lower classes lived side by side in the inner town area.

As the century developed the wealthier amongst the population had moved away from the smoke-filled centre towards the fresh air and wider open spaces of the outer suburbs. The lower classes remained in the south, Quarry Hill area of the city whilst the middle classes populated the west and north. However, all but the wealthy

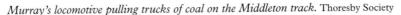

Murray's locomotive pulling trucks of coal on the Middleton track. Thoresby Society

still lived within walking distance of Briggate. Those with more money, who lived further out, travelled into Leeds either on foot, or by using their own vehicles. Many had their own carriages although some hired a hackney coach, a popular mode of transport which first came to Leeds in April 1824.

A horse-drawn tramway system was first constructed in Leeds in 1871 and was triggered by the Tramways Act of the previous year which signalled a boost to this mode of transport. A short piece of track was laid on some vacant land in Cookridge Street and a private company established the first route to Headingley in 1871. Further services soon followed, to Chapeltown, Kirkstall, Hunslet and Marsh Lane.

More routes followed and eventually steam trams took over from the over-worked horses before electrification became established as the nineteenth century drew to a close. The first electric tramway opened in 1891 when a length of line nearly two miles in length was laid from Sheepscar to Roundhay Park. At the time it was the first electrically driven tram service in Britain. This line led to the growth in popularity of Roundhay Park, which in the previous twenty years since its opening had been seen to be something of a white elephant by the people of Leeds who were aware of its existence, but unable to travel to it.

A significant boost to the tramway system in Leeds came when the Corporation bought it. Fares were kept to a minimum and there were early morning concessions for factory workers. A two-mile journey cost just a penny and neighbouring towns were linked to the network enabling people to travel further afield.

There was also a route-numbering scheme with each terminus having a unique number making it easier for passengers to identify the routes. The number twenty-seven terminated near to the cricket and rugby ground at Headingley and quickly became essential transport to spectators when arriving at and leaving the ground.

Trams extended their routes during the 1930s as new housing estates sprouted up around the city. New bogie cars were developed specifically for a new route to serve the Belle Isle housing development. However, though Leeds still had a tram system when many other cities had consigned theirs to the memory books, they were finally phased out in the 1950s with the last tramcar running in Leeds on 7 November 1959.

Railways
Leeds held the advantage of having the oldest horse-drawn railroad in the world. Built in 1758, the three and a half mile railroad supplied

North-Eastern Railway Viaduct. It linked railway termini on opposite sides of Leeds. The author

the people of Leeds with coal from the Middleton Colliery and signalled the beginning of railways in this country, half a century before the mode of transport began in earnest.

The 1758 Middleton Railway Trust first began with a wagonway linking Charles Brandling's coal pits to the coal staith at Casson Close near to Leeds Bridge. John Blenkinsop came to Middleton as manager around 1808 and commissioned Matthew Murray to build a steam engine on a test track at the Round Foundry. The engine was finally tried on the wagonway on 24 June 1812.

Murray's engine was the first commercially successful steam locomotive in the world when it commenced operation on the Middleton Railway. Included in the design was the Blenkinsop rack

Leeds Bridge as it stands today. The author

and pinion drive, which was the first regular revenue-earning use of steam traction, as distinct from experimental operation, in the world.

During the 1820s there was a major rail project in the north of England with the laying of separate sets of tracks between Leeds and Selby, Hull and Manchester. The owners of the Aire and Calder Navigation realised they were sitting on a potential goldmine as they could bypass the canal network by carrying the goods to Selby and then transfer it onto boats for the journey onto Hull.

In September 1834 the Leeds to Selby railway opened for the transport of passengers and goods. It was announced that the public could be accommodated with places and three of the first-class and six of the second-class carriages were filled with passengers. The first journey saw the number of people travelling number 200 and there

Leeds Bridge House. The author

were police and other officials stationed on different parts of the line to ensure that order was maintained. The papers of the time report that the initial journey went off without a hitch:

Former offices of the Aire and Calder Navigation. The author

> *save a little fear and consternation put upon some horses, pigs and geese which we passed at various points and a cow which jumped over a five-part gate to get out of the way.*

It later emerged that an accident did occur on one of the first journeys made along the Leeds to Selby route when a man called John Kepper who either through being careless or drunk, was lying by the side of the tracks. As a train approached he was unable to get out of the way and the engine passed over his right arm, severing it from his body.

Two years after the line opened, in 1836, Parliament gave permission for the line to be extended from Selby to Hull and the thirty-one mile long line was opened in 1840. The Leeds & Selby line remained independent until 1844 when the York & North Midland

Railway bought it. Though it was criticised for being slow at the beginning, it was soon to become a great success carrying 3,500 passengers and a great amount of freight every week.

In 1837 Parliament gave permission for the building of a railway between Manchester and Leeds, though George Stephenson, the chief engineer, had several problems to overcome on the fifty-one mile long line across the Pennines. The most difficult of these was the Summit Tunnel, which was over a mile long.

It was eventually opened in 1839 and branches were built to Heywood, Oldham and Halifax. However, here too, there were difficulties with particular problems being experienced during the construction of the three-mile Woodhead Tunnel on the line to Sheffield, which was not completed until 1845. Thirty-two navvies were killed and 140 were seriously injured during the building of the tunnel.

The completion of the Manchester & Leeds Railway enabled passengers to travel by rail across most of the north of England and was crucial to the development of both Manchester and Leeds during the Industrial Revolution. This line was in 1847 to become the principal constituent of the Lancashire and Yorkshire Railway. Leeds was now linked to Liverpool on the West Coast and to the East Coast at Goole on the River Humber.

Leeds had to have railway stations to cope with the passenger traffic coming into the town and the first passenger train pulled into Marsh Lane station in Leeds on 22 September 1834. By 1840 the North Midland Railway opened a second line from a terminus at Hunslet Lane to link Leeds with the Midlands and London.

The Leeds and Bradford Railway opened a link along the Aire Valley and created a third Leeds station on Wellington Street. Completed in 1857 it was named the Central Station.

In 1869 the North Eastern Railway extended its line from Marsh Lane to a new terminus near to the Wellington Street Station and by 1938 these two stations were combined with the new station becoming known as Leeds City Station.

Sea travel

Leeds had a good trade with the American colonies and before the War of Independence many advertisements promoted vessels sailing from England to American ports. The export of cloth and other goods was large.

Leeds also had hopes of being regarded as a major port at one time and some vessels including the *Pioneer* were often seen arriving on the

River Aire. These hopes were advanced in 1911 when the steam ship *Coronation* arrived in the city. The most powerful vessel of its kind, it docked at The Calls on its maiden voyage. The *Yorkshire Evening Post* commented:

> *The Pioneer no longer ploughs her way through the inky waters of the evil smelling Aire, but there are now several more vessels of similar design which regularly bring cargoes as far as Leeds Bridge.*

The *Coronation*, however, was a more powerful vessel altogether being a tug as well as a steamer. When it arrived in Leeds it was carrying 105 tonnes of flour. With the Manchester Ship Canal having become a success there were hopes until well into the twentieth century of creating a Leeds Ship Canal to link the city with the sea. However, with the reduction of coal transport by water the plan never materialised and the improvements to the road system saw Leeds committed to improving transport on land.

Road transport was greatly advanced by the first motor car, which was constructed in 1897 by Messrs Dougill. It was driven by one of the firm's ordinary gas engines and power was transmitted to the driving wheels by belts running on different sized pulleys. The car was capable of a maximum speed of about eighteen miles an hour and only had two speeds, forwards and reverse though it did have an automatic ignition.

As the roads developed to accommodate the growing number of cars on the roads of Leeds, the first permanent traffic lights in Britain were installed in Park Row in 1928. Motorway travel was not too far behind and the M1 came to Leeds in December 1972 upon the completion of the section from Stourton; the M62 came a little later.

4   *D*IET

In medieval times the peasants in Leeds lived by cultivating their ridge and furrow strips of land in the open fields and by grazing sheep and cattle. They supplemented their diet by small amounts of vegetables and dairy products produced on nearby land. Wheat and rye were grown for bread, oats for porridge and oatcakes and barley for brewing beer. Peas and beans were grown as a crop from the fourteenth century onwards and other vegetables were also grown on adjoining fields.

Hens, pigs, sheep, goats and cows were also kept as meat and the by-products of milk, butter, cheese and eggs were important elements of a peasant's diet. The agricultural area to the east of Leeds ensured that the town was well supplied with local produce.

In Georgian Leeds the diet of the lower classes depended largely upon the season with more food available during the summer and autumn months when the crops were reaped. Oatcakes were still an important part of the average diet along with bread, milk and porridge. Meat was on the menu a couple of times a week though the more affluent workers were able to afford meat, especially beef and mutton a little more often.

In 1797 Sir Frederick Eden wrote a report on 'The state of the Poor', which gave an insight into the diet of many of the labouring people as the town moved into the nineteenth century:

Tea is now the ordinary breakfast, especially among women of every description, and the food of both men and women is more expensive than that consumed by persons in the same station of life in the more northern parts. Many persons complain that the introduction of machinery for spinning and carding wool not only deprive the industrious poor of employment but are a great national disadvantage. But the high price of land and water, the many new streets in the town, and the manufactories and villas in the neighbourhood are a very convincing proof of the prosperity of Leeds.

Griffith Wright provided a poem which gave a further glimpse into the diet in a mid-eighteenth century household of a Leeds clothier:

'Ere clocks strikes eight they're called to breakfast and bowls of milk are brought in great haste good water pudding as heart could wish comes spoons stuck round an earthen dish.

At midday with wooden platter, bowl and laden All seated round a scoured table.

Hard oaten cakes some two or three in pieces fly with fist and knee.

Tho hard it in an instant doth Eat like soft manchet in the broth On earthen dish with leg of mutton As good a knife was ever put in.

The rhyme also referred to a broth, which would have been served in the evening, with a sheep's head as the main ingredient. People went to the Shambles area of the town and came away with a sackful of sheep's heads which would be boiled in a large pot along with bacon. This was the forerunner of golden guinea broth which was a popular dish for both breakfast and dessert.

Oatcakes, butter, milk, eggs and a cheese made out of skimmed or blue milk were the staple diet of many people during the early part of the 1800s. At harvest time great quantities of oatcakes had to be made for the labourers to feast upon. When soft and fresh the cakes were eaten with butter or treacle and rolled up. This was a particular favourite with children.

Oatcakes were versatile and were also used as a savoury dish. They could be made into sops with portions being soaked in gravy in the gravy tin under the roasting beef. In Leeds, all the public houses which provided meals, always gave oatcakes and dripping free, the dripping generally being fresh and warm from the joint.

The Shambles, Briggate. Author's collection

By the end of the nineteenth century there were shops selling oatcakes in most towns in the country including Leeds. These would be owned by specialist bakers who would install large cast-iron bakestones. The bakers would also sell crumpets, muffins and milk cakes.

Israel Roberts, in his autobiography about life in Leeds in the 1800s said:

Wheat bread in those days was a luxury rarely indulged in and a diet for the poor, I am told, was chiefly oatmeal in porridge and cake with potatoes and cornbread, which was nearly as hard as a stone. And those who could procure a little bacon now and then were very fortunate.

In some towns, cheap and wholesome flour was produced by setting up co-operative mills and by 1847 the Leeds Flour Society had been founded. In return for the payment of a guinea, members could buy enough flour to feed themselves and their family.

Other families took a more risky strategy in trying to procure a better diet for their families. In Leeds pigs were often kept in garden plots or on allotments and occasionally within the courtyards of the centre of town.

One visitor to the east of Leeds in the 1840s mentioned how he:

plodded by the half hour through streets in which the undisturbed mud lay in wreaths from wall to wall, across open spaces, overlooked by houses all around, in which the pigs, wandering from their central oasis, seemed to be roaming through what was only a large sty.

Pigs in fact were more common in some areas of Leeds than cats or dogs. The inhabitants of the cellar dwellings in Leeds sometimes shared their space with the pigs which made their homes in the corner of the cellar. The pig excrement had to be carried up the steps from the cellar before being thrown into the street and it wasn't until local government finally began to fight dirt and disease in the 1870s and 1880s that pigs were finally removed from the town centre. However, pig keeping remained popular with families saving every scrap of household waste to feed to the pig in order to fatten them up.

For those who were able to afford meat, the butchers of Leeds ensured a good supply of livestock. In the nineteenth century Leeds butchers set off from town on horseback or in gigs early in the morning to make their way to country markets so that they could buy in some stock. Some occasionally went as far north as Morpeth to try and buy in better quality produce. Any cattle they bought at the markets had to be transported back to Leeds by road and on arrival in Leeds the cattle would usually be on show for a while in pens on the market side of old Vicar Lane.

The Shambles, consisting of two or three rows of ramshackle huts and shanties between Briggate and Vicar Lane, was the centre of the Leeds meat industry. At the end of one of the rows in the Shambles was a dancing saloon and at the other was a religious meeting room and both were regularly used by the butchers. It was a close community and when a butcher in the Shambles died, his comrades would attend the funeral in their working clothes, merely substituting their flat caps for tall silk hats.

One of the butchers, William Jackson, was known as 'Bull Bill'. A big man with a huge voice, he mainly traded in bulls hence his nickname. He prided himself on being an expert driver and became notorious for steering his 'tit' and trap between the posts of the Briggate end of the Shambles before drawing up at the door of his stand.

By the time of the Industrial Revolution many people were flocking into Leeds with the promise of plentiful employment. With the many back to backs being built all around the town, conditions were grim for many and their diet was usually no better than their living conditions. A typical shopping basket for a week would include stone flour for bread, eggs, yeast, milk, stone oatmeal, treacle, sugar, tea, coffee, meat, vegetables, salt, pepper, mustard, vinegar and beer.

All people drank large amounts of tea, but there the similarities between the working classes and those who were more affluent ended. In Victorian times the diet of the average working man was poor. Porridge still formed the staple breakfast along with bread and dripping and a cup of tea. Dinner was similar though those with more income may have been able to stretch to a little meat and boiled potatoes. However, working class families were fortunate if they sat down to a meal including meat twice a week.

The situation was not as dire for the middle classes who were able to afford fish, meat, including roast beef and legs of mutton and vegetables as well as wines. A middle class family may well have been dining on the likes of broth with dumplings, rabbit stew or corned beef hash.

The wealthy who lived outside of the inner areas of Leeds also had the advantage of living off the land and traditionally, Yorkshire eggs and bacon were the favoured breakfast dish for yeoman farmers or statesmen of rural areas. Another breakfast favourite was thickly sliced bacon or hams, home cured and served with oatcakes or bread with strong tea as an accompaniment.

Whilst the diet of the working classes was generally poor, it was worse for the unemployed, or those not in regular jobs. They had to make do with bread and tea, with meat just being a very occasional treat.

To illustrate this surgeon Robert Baker carried out a survey of the labouring classes in Leeds in the late 1830s and recounted a conversation he had with a group of Irish factory children:

When have you had flesh meat?
Whenever we get it, sometimes once a week.
What then do you live upon?
Coffee and bread or tea.

Working men, whilst they may have struggled with a poor diet at home, at least had some other ways of getting a hot meal during the working day. The 1800s saw the advent of Working Men's Institutes which were popular dining places for those workers able to afford them and they provided the working man with a cooked meal. Steaks, chops and bacon were generally on the menu along with bread and butter or muffins, washed down with tea or coffee.

With the spread of industry during the nineteenth century there was a great need for immediate food for working men who were not able to get home for lunch and as a result, as well as the Working Men's Institutes, pie shops became established in Leeds. There were such shops surviving in the city long after the end of the Second World War as the demand was apparent for 'summat hot and filling among the working classes'.

The people of Leeds also became used to eating on the move during Victorian times as street vendors started to become a familiar sight. Hot pea sellers would serve mushy peas in a mint sauce, with chips, cockles, muffins, roast potatoes and hokey pokey, a predecessor of ice cream, also being sold.

Food on the move was especially popular at carnivals and fairs in Leeds. On entering the main fair in Leeds, the thousands of visitors would pass the 'Original Pea Shop' or 'Uncle Tom's Cabin Pea Shop' which sold boiled peas. They were served on a small plate with a flavouring of vinegar, salt and pepper.

The Victorian working class diet was dependent upon supply and was basic as a consequence. Relatively few had ovens, having to rely

Hunslet Feast showing Hunslet Church in the background. Thoresby Society

either on open-fire pan cooking, buying their hot food out, or making do with cold meals. Many families only possessed one pot and had to use that for many other purposes besides cooking!

Primitive cooking facilities combined with a lack of cheap fuel, poverty, ignorance, and adulterated foods to produce a Victorian Britain which contained an underclass seriously undernourished.

The contrast between the middle and working classes was stark and this was demonstrated even more clearly when Queen Victoria and Prince Albert opened the Leeds Town Hall on 7 September 1858. The opening was marked by the first Leeds Music Festival and to round off the occasion, the Queen and her husband accompanied 272 distinguished guests at a celebration banquet.

The meal included twenty quarts of turtle soup, beef, veal and ham, five game pies, two boar's heads, twenty lobsters and nine turkeys, roast fowl, grouse, pigeon and pheasants to be followed by specially imported pineapples, grapes, peaches, apricots, apples and

Leeds Town Hall. The author

pears. The meal was washed down by 114 decanters of the best hock, champagne, clarets and other wines.

Fine wines were not part of the working man's diet but beer certainly was and home-brewed beers were important as well as desirable. As a great deal of weight could be lost in the furnaces and coalmines, a lot of liquid had to be consumed, sometimes about twenty pints. For this reason the beer was watered down as to not do so would have left the men unfit for work the next day!

In some factories during the latter half of the nineteenth century beer was provided for workers by the management. At the Yorkshire Copper Works in Leeds a barrel of beer from the brewery was given each week to the men in the foundry. Drinking competitions were a regular feature between companies.

By the latter years of the nineteenth century the diet of the working man began to improve slightly. Between 1877 and 1889 the cost of the average national weekly food basket of butter, bread, tea, milk and meat fell by about thirty per cent and the nation began to see some first signs of nutritional improvement with a greater variety of foods and new methods of retailing.

However, to those in lower paid jobs or who were struggling to bring in a wage, the improvements were not immediately apparent. Bread and treacle was a typical breakfast for a child in a working class family, whilst the main meal of the day usually comprised of a cheaper cut of meat, often black pudding or liver and onions. Many families still had no meat at all during the week, before having a 'Sunday joint' at the weekend. Such limits tested the cooking skills of families in these situations and often people were able to make a little go a relatively long way.

Many survived on bread and butter with jam, occasionally supplemented with cheap cuts of meat with eggs and bacon, a treat reserved solely for Sunday mornings. Some people sampled the delights of Nestle's milk spread onto bread, often with sugar sprinkled on top of it. Others who could not afford real gravy or even some meat dissolved an Oxo cube in hot water to make gravy and then use it to dip their bread into.

Desserts were served a couple of times a week and tended to be rice pudding or rhubarb pies. Bread and butter and a pot of tea were an essential part of any meal, and were also served at tea times. The last meal of the day was supper and this would consist of bread, butter and cheese, cold meat or fish.

Sunday roast

In the nineteenth century the family became separated by the working week, leaving only Sunday as a day for the family to spend together with Sunday lunchtime becoming one of the few times in the week when the family could all be around the same table sharing a meal, after church, chapel or Sunday school. The meal usually began by the serving of a Yorkshire pudding with gravy followed by the roast with potatoes and vegetables. If families were choosing not to eat beef, they were likely to be eating baked ham or roasted rabbit.

Later in the day, at about five o'clock, tea would be served with cold meats, bread and butter and cakes. Over the few days after Sunday, the meat from the roast reappeared at dinner times when it was served cold with potatoes and perhaps with a little beetroot or pickle. The last of the meat would appear in a sort of hash by the middle of the week and many families would then be left with cheaper meats such as bacon or without meat for two or three days until Sunday came round again.

Christmas in Leeds

Christmas-time, always a time of religious worship, was also, as it is today, a time of the year for eating and making merry. Christmas in Leeds during Victorian times saw the shop windows in the centre of town bristling with holly and bright colours and Leeds grocers, 'had achieved wondrous compositions by the aid of huge eaves of currants and raisins, piles of golden oranges and boxes of fruit'.

Superior pieces of beef and mutton, especially for the festive season hung in butcher's shops and the sight of turkeys and game suspended against their fronts largely concealed many of the poulterer's and gamedealers shops.

It was customary for families on the eve of the twelfth day of Christmas to invite their relatives, friends and neighbours round to their house to play cards and have supper. Mince pies and a plate of spiced caked would often be handed round as was a wassail bowl. Everyone took a roasted apple out of the ale with a spoon and then ate it and drank the ale, wishing everyone a merry Christmas and a happy new year. The ingredients of the bowl were ale, sugar, nutmeg and roasted apples, known as lambs-wool.

The Christmas dinner itself began with a type of large Yorkshire pudding, though this was made with mixed herbs and was known as 'savoury pudding'. It was served separately and after the traditional turkey and plum pudding, a Christmas tea was served with pork pie, boiled ham, cheese, jellies, trifles and Christmas cake.

Home-grown produce

As Leeds entered the industrial age, markets in the city became more important as sources of cheap food to feed the masses who descended on the West Riding. Rhubarb was a highly localised crop grown in Yorkshire and which has flourished in Leeds since the time of the Industrial Revolution.

Growing concentrated in this area due to climatic conditions along with good marketing outlets and communications. During the nineteenth century the 'Rhubarb for Charity' was a popular annual event in rhubarb growing areas around Leeds. The event would be organised by the congregation of a chapel and would meet to share food. Usually there was a large tea of home-made dishes, always including pies and stewed rhubarb.

There would also be music including a local band and a sing-a-long by everyone in the room. Finally, there would be a collection of money to be distributed among local charities.

All kinds of fish were sold in markets throughout Leeds as early as the sixteenth century. From earliest times fish was in plentiful supply, mainly freshwater and large fishponds were constructed, enabling fish to be farmed. During the seventeenth century a writer gave his account of Leeds:

Rhubarb flower, Leeds is a popular growing area. The author

Central Market in Leeds. Thoresby Society

Kirkgate market. Author's collection

> *Above the market of the milk cows was the ichthyopolium, which not withstanding its great distance from the sea, was weekly twice or thrice, if not oftener, plentifully furnished with great variety of fish.*

Rabbits were often found on the wide moors and fields of Yorkshire until myxomatosis struck and were the only source of fresh meat for many people. However, until game laws became stricter in the late nineteenth century, wild geese and almost any imaginable sort of birdlife was deemed fit for the dining table. Goose, pigeon, duck and game of all kinds were used in the making of the traditional Yorkshire Christmas pies of the eighteenth century. These were also widely sent as gifts during the festive season.

5 *H*EALTH

D uring the sixteenth and early seventeenth century, buildings in Leeds were largely half-timbered jettied houses but these were replaced from the seventeenth century onwards to brick built cloth merchants houses. The best surviving examples are in Queens Court and Lambert's Yard. However, as the population of the town began to grow, so did the insanitary conditions in which people lived.

Queens Court. An example of seventeenth century merchants housing. The author

In 1604 York suffered dreadfully from the bubonic plague with 3,000 fatalities. It was too close not to have an effect on Leeds and the disease soon swept south, badly affecting the town. The regular market in Leeds was closed down immediately and alternative ones were established on Hunslet and Chapeltown Moors. These were ticket only events and traders had to have a signed certificate stating that they were free from infection.

More than once the people of Leeds succumbed to the bubonic plague. During 1644 and 1645 there were further outbreaks in Beeston and Holbeck. The poor, overcrowded areas of the inner city were more susceptible to the disease and it soon spread in these parts of town, though the comparatively open spaces of the outskirts were also affected.

Between March and Christmas Day of 1645 1,325 people in Leeds died due to the plague, about one-fifth of the population at that time. It originally struck in Vicar Lane and spread quickly through Leeds and on out to the townships. The disease was on the wane the year after, but the town took some time to recover. Houses had to be fumigated and less valuable items destroyed.

An example of the overcrowded conditions in Leeds at the end of the nineteenth century. Thoresby Society

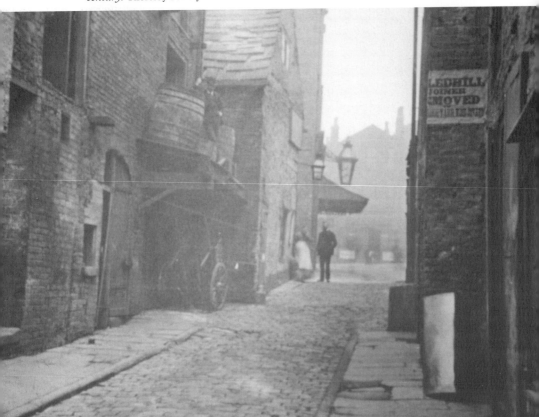

People of influence in Leeds did take steps to improve the public health of the town and it became one of the first towns in Britain to have a piped water supply to houses. This came into operation in 1694 and was designed by the engineers George Sorocold and Henry Gilbert. A water wheel built near Leeds Bridge, Lower Briggate, pumped water from the River Aire through lead pipes to a storage reservoir – or 'cistern' – in Wade Lane, where it served the wealthier inhabitants in a town, which at that stage numbered 7,000. In 1755 the corporation obtained an act for the purpose of providing light and for the paving of the main streets.

By 1801, the year of the first census, the population of Leeds had reached 30,000 and by the standards of the time it was a large town. However, it was spreading rapidly and many of the new houses built were dreadful. Overcrowding was rife and the streets were very dirty.

In the 1850s the council built sewers but many of the houses in Leeds were not connected to them, so many dwellings continued to use cesspits or buckets which were emptied at night by the 'night soil' men. Not until 1899 was it made compulsory for dwellings to be connected to sewers.

Ship Yard, an example of inner-city streets at the beginning of the twentieth century.
Thoresby Society

The Leeds of the 1830s presented an industrial panorama dominated by textile mills. The skyline bristled with tall chimneys belching their smoke and attendant lung diseases onto a largely helpless population. The factory owners and middle classes, who lived to the west and on the hillsides of Woodhouse or Headingley, were not as badly affected, protected as they were, from the swirling smog caused by the prevailing westerly winds.

Crowded into the terraces and tenements in the heart of the township were the working classes. In consequence of the furious expansion of industry, the population of Leeds had increased from 30,000 in 1801 to 67,000 in 1831. To cater for this influx of people unscrupulous landowners had crammed dwellings into every imaginable nook and cranny. Very few of the streets and yards were paved or drained.

The result was that only in dry weather could the inhabitants walk the streets without sinking ankle deep in mud. Domestic and human waste would be deposited in the street: sometimes in designated middenheaps, which only occasionally would be be cleared by scavengers. Stagnant pools in the streets were a common feature and at times the stench was unbearable. The insanitary conditions in the street inevitably spilled into the dwellings.

It was from these quarters that cholera hit Leeds during the national epidemic of 1832. Cholera swept across Europe in 1831 and soon reached the shores of England, though it was another year before it infiltrated Leeds. The first victim in Leeds – in May of that year – was the child of a weaver living in a five and a half yard square cottage in Blue Bell Fold which was near Marsh Lane. With good reason the disease was called 'King Cholera' – having more the aspect of an almighty curse than a plain disease. It had spread rapidly since the first case was recorded in Sunderland with the victims afflicted by a violent pain in the stomach, followed by diarrhoea, sickness and eventually death.

Once the disease reached Leeds it quickly spread to those areas of town which were particularly affected by overcrowding and poor sanitary conditions. A cholera hospital was established in St Peter's Square but in a six-month period, of the 1,817 cases of cholera in Leeds, over 700 died. The epidemic was so deadly that a special cholera graveyard was built on Mabgate west of the site of St Mary's Church at Quarry Hill.

Other diseases affected many of those who did not succumb to cholera. Typhus hit Leeds in 1847 whilst in 1849 there were occasional outbreaks of smallpox, scarlet fever and typhoid fever.

Cholera returned in 1848 killing about 2,000 people in Leeds alone and in 1865 there was another big outbreak of typhus with about 600 patients admitted to the House of Recovery. Although the disease was centred in the working class areas, the middle and upper classes were affected too and panic set in amongst the population at large, seemingly incapable of stemming the flow of deadly diseases which were regularly targeting Leeds.

Many families all over town were hit by disease and there was fear amongst the public that their house would be next. The public generally had little knowledge of cholera or disease generally; indeed many people thought that disease was transmitted by smells! Koch's discovery of the microbe had yet to be made and most of the cures and preventative measures of the time did not work.

It was the academics of the town who made the link between disease and living conditions. Robert Baker, a Leeds surgeon, who was later to become embroiled in the resurrectionist's controversy of the nineteenth century, undertook a series of reports to look into disease in Leeds and he focussed on the slum areas of the town as being particularly prevalent in attracting epidemics. He studied the marked geographical pattern to disease which showed that the worst hit areas were the poor areas to the east of the town centre. In particular, there was shown to be a clear link between disease and poor drainage and the eventual report was sent to the Home Secretary in London. Baker wrote:

The surface of these streets is considerably elevated by accumulated ashes and filth, untouched by any scavenger; they form the nuclei of disease exhaled from a thousand sources. Here and there stagnant water, and channels so offensive that they have been declared to be unbearable, lie under the doorways of the uncomplaining poor; and privies so laden with ashes and excrementitious matter, as to be unuseable, prevail, till the streets themselves become offensive from deposits of this description: in short there is generally pervading these localities a want of the common conveniences of life.

The cholera epidemic of 1832 had led, a year later, to a joint declaration by six physicians and thirty-eight surgeons that the future health of the people of Leeds depended upon a great improvement in drainage, sewage and paving and better regulations on cleaning the streets.

However the words of the joint declaration appeared to fall on deaf ears and many people still threw much of their waste into the street whilst others insisted on keeping livestock, especially pigs in their yards or even in their houses. This was done in order to supplement the family diet, however it added greatly to the public hygiene problems affecting Leeds at the time. Dr Robert Baker gave an example:

> *In one of the streets an expiring Irish woman was found in a cellar dwelling surrounded by her family and a number of pigs, the filth of which latter it would be necessary to remove into the street by hand. The houses were often unclean and ill-ventilated and people often shared a bed.*

Any spare land which had not been built upon was seen as suitable 'dumping grounds' for the population during the nineteenth century. Pigsties were often erected upon these sites and they were described as 'depots of dung' by the much-gatherers. 341 people were living in fifty-seven rooms in Boot and Shoe Yard in Leeds in 1837 and it was from the same yard that seventy cartloads of manure had been removed five years earlier. The yard was eventually demolished to make way for an extension to Kirkgate market.

A report noted that:

Dock Street containing some of the last remaining back to back houses in Leeds city centre. The author

Three parallel streets, which are neither sewered, drained, paved or cleansed ... occupied entirely by cottage dwellings with cellar dwellings also for a population ... of 386 persons, there are but 2 simple privies and these are in such a state as to be totally unavailable.

Another report in 1842 noted that in a typical Irish weaver's cottage in Leeds:

The kitchen is not only appropriated to culinary purposes, but is the house, the sleeping room, the hen house, and the piggery; whilst upstairs are three or four looms all but touching each other; perhaps, in a corner, a bed on the floor for one of the owners of these looms.

It was felt that the keeping of livestock was at the heart of the problem and the authorities resolved to take draconian action against those keeping animals such as pigs in their homes. However, people fought back and the Leeds Pig Protection Society was formed in 1866 to defend people it considered to be badly treated by the town council. Several people complained about what they felt was a 'crusade against the pigs in Leeds' and argued that keeping animals was not a public nuisance.

Many people sought the backing of the society after they received a summons for creating a nuisance by keeping a pig-sty. In all such cases the decision of the bench was that the keeping of pigs was a nuisance and a risk to the health of the human population living in the vicinity. It ordered that the animals must be removed within seven days.

However, sharing homes with livestock was only the tip of the iceberg. Even where drainage was available in Victorian Leeds, it left a great deal to be desired. It was common in the early Victorian towns for the sewers to be chiefly flat bottomed passages and conduits, laid in a piecemeal fashion, with inadequate gradients. These sewers were totally unsuitable for the mixture of rainwater, waste water and excrement which they received. The flat bottoms and shallow slopes ensured that they soon became choked up with all manner of unpleasant and unhealthy accumulations.

At the beginning of the nineteenth century sewerage did not distress the minds of people as it would today. Each block of houses had a cess pool to which sewage filtered by means of square drains of stone. However, there was no public drainage to speak of.

The material deposited in this manner gave rise to poisonous gases such as methane, which would often find its way into the houses through untrapped drains. Even the wealthy houses were affected, according to evidence given to a House of Commons Committee in 1834, but it was the servants sleeping in the 'lower rooms' who took the brunt of the resulting ill health!

In the early years of the nineteenth century the waterworks company was only supplying about 2,000 houses and most of the inhabitants of Leeds relied instead on wells, boreholes, water-carriers and the River Aire. This had an adverse effect on the river which, by 1830, was completely unsafe for drinking. According to a piece in the *Leeds Intelligencer* in 1841 it was:

> ... *charged with the contents of about 200 water closets and similar places, a great number of common drains, the drainings from dunghills, the Infirmary (dead leeches, poultices for patients, etc), slaughter houses, chemical soap, gas, dung, dyehouses and manufacturies, spent blue and black dye, pig manure, old urine wash, with all sorts of decomposed animal and vegetable substances from an extent of drainage between Armley Mills to the Kings Mill amounting to about 30,000,000 gallons per annum of the mass of filth with which the river is loaded.*

The Leeds Waterworks Company discontinued its use of the Aire for drinking water in 1841 and used instead, as a temporary supply, the

Leeds Burial Ground opened due to the population growth of the nineteenth century. The author

water leaking into the partially complete tunnel linking Leeds with the proposed Eccup reservoir.

A permanent water supply in Leeds was still desperately needed and the town was fortunate in having many springs from where the outlying districts were able to source their water. Holbeck had spaw water and many residents were familiar with the sight of barrel shaped carts which went round many neighbourhoods accompanied by the cry 'Holbeck spaw watter', which was popular as it was more suitable for drinking and making tea.

With the conditions in which the vast majority of the population were living, it was little wonder that the death rate in Leeds rose from twenty per thousand in 1831 to twenty-seven per thousand in 1841. In 1845 another report into the living conditions of many of the population stated that infant mortality was high with the proportion of infant deaths under five years old to total deaths being thirty and a half per cent. The report said that a number of dwellings in the Leeds area were unhealthy, largely due to the 'decaying matter at the bottom of the Beck' combined with the smoke and fumes which were a by-product of Leeds during the Industrial Revolution.

The report said that the worst types of housing were the yards where 'ashes, garbage and filth of all kinds are thrown from the doors and windows of the houses upon the surface of the streets and courts'. It added:

The feelings of people are blunted to all seeming decency, and from the constantly contaminated state of the atmosphere, a vast amount of ill health prevails, leading to listlessness, and inducing a desire for spirits and opiates; the combined influence of the whole condition causing much loss of time, increasing poverty, and terminating the existence of many in premature death.

Many of the problems Leeds was facing were a direct result of the Industrial Revolution which in turn had clearly led to something of a 'revolution' in the town. Production became concentrated around the factories in Leeds and working people had to crowd into congested and generally unhealthy districts which had been hurriedly built to house them.

Living in the same neighbourhood as the factories in which they worked led to further health problems, notably smoke pollution. Dr Turner Thackrah wrote a paper on the subject saying that he doubted whether ten per cent of the population enjoyed full health. He added that the air of the town was always in an unnatural state:

The excess of carbonic acid gas is said to be very trifling, but our skins and linen prove an abundant mixture of charcoal itself. Ammoniacal under the vapours from manufactories, sewers and places of refuse add to the general impurity. This state of the atmosphere affects to a greater or lesser degree all the inhabitants. The complexion is pallid and the tongue shows that the digestion is disordered and imperfect.

Smoke pollution led to further difficulties within the town as plants would not grow and the gardens in the Leeds area suffered.

Throughout the second half of the nineteenth century, the Government, in a bid to react to the problem, began to push through a series of Public Health acts and the issue captured the attention of many in Leeds too. Mrs Emily Kitson, a member of the Yorkshire Ladies Council, told a lecture in 1873 that a large proportion of the death rate in Leeds was due to preventable illnesses such as fevers and she warned the members present of ill-ventilated rooms.

She added that in Mann's Field there was masses of new housing and new streets without a drain of any kind and that the area was surrounded by pools of stagnant water, a breeding ground for cholera.

Concern about the deteriorating physical health of the population was mounting and it came to a head when during recruiting for the Boer War between 1899 and 1902, the men were seen to be in generally poor health, news that shocked and alarmed the authorities.

This ensured that the health of the general public continued to be an issue as the nineteenth century drew to a close though the Education Act of 1870 which provided compulsory elementary education also helped as it highlighted the issue of the poor domestic conditions of many children. The act drew a clear distinction between children and the workforce and they began to be treated less like young adults and more like the vulnerable children they often were, requiring the protection of the law.

In 1905 Dr William Hall from Leeds made a study of nutrition amongst Leeds children and together with the Yorkshire Ladies Council he tried to establish, unsuccessfully as it turned out, a depot to provide free milk suitable for babies. This was necessary as milk was a health hazard at the time.

Inspection of cow herds was inadequate and transportation from country to town was slow and unrefrigerated. Patent foods for babies were often harmful as they contained insufficient fat and protein and too much starch. Tins of condensed milk, also used for babies, were regularly left open for flies to get to. The large use of horses for road transport also led to a ready supply of flies and in the summer month's epidemics of infant diarrhoea took a heavy toll.

The infant death rate in Leeds for the year ending 1 January 1911 was 123 deaths per thousand. Sixty per cent of schoolchildren were in some way deficient and out of every thousand babies born in Leeds only about 340 healthy children went to school. An appeal from Leeds Babies' Welcome said:

> *Looking at Leeds streets with seeing eyes, the bent legs, stunted growth, weak eyes, etc of the workpeople as they pore out of the factories, and the ambulances with their pitiful load of children on crutches, it is not hard to believe that half the adults of the new generation are in some way maimed. This is more terrible than the death of infants. We citizens of Leeds should be made to feel the shame of it for it has been demonstrated over and over again that much of this disease is easily preventable.*

The constant threat of fevers and other epidemics opened many peoples' eyes to the need to have a building to where people could be removed from the impure air surrounding them. The House of Recovery was designed for this purpose, but it was built within the confines of the town in Vicar Lane, so by 1884 it was decided to relocate to a healthier part of the town, slightly further away from the smoke and grime which coated inner Leeds. The House of Recovery settled in Beckett Street before being bought by the Leeds Corporation as a fever hospital a year later.

In July 1767 the decision was made to build an infirmary in Leeds. The new hospital, which was based in Kirkgate, was built due to a donation of £5,000 from the townsfolk and was small, having a capacity for just three in-patients and the same number of out-patients. Its principal founder, William Hey was one of the outstanding surgeons of the eighteenth century.

In the 1820s the infirmary and the House of Recovery were complemented by new institutions such as the new Ear and Eye infirmary and a lying-in hospital for poor married women. Emphasis was being placed increasingly on people being treated as out-patients as the hospitals struggled to cope with the increasing population, leading to a chronic shortage of beds.

In 1824 the Leeds Public Dispensary opened its doors in part of the House of Recovery. It was a primitive system at first as one of the trustees had to vouch for patients before they were allowed to receive treatment, although exceptions were made in cases of emergency.

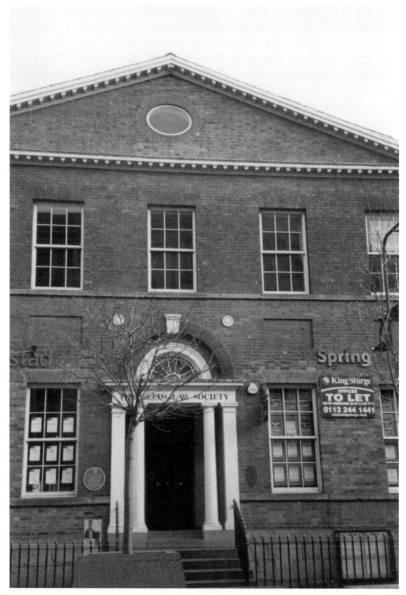

William Hey's house, the founder of the General Infirmary. The author

A few years later, in 1831, the Leeds Medical School was founded by a group of surgeons and doctors. Initially they hired rooms in the Dispensary on the corner of Templar Street and Vicar Lane. The school was one of the first provincial medical schools in the country

The original Leeds Infirmary. Thoresby Society

Leeds School of Medicine. The author

and in 1834 the school was moved to East Parade. A new school, built in Park Street was opened on 3 October 1865.

By this time the demand for medical care had risen in line with the population growth and Leeds General Infirmary was too small to cope with the demand. In 1860 planning started for a new block of buildings at the present site on Great George Street. Work started on the new building which was built to a design by Sir George Gilbert Scott in a medieval gothic style and the legendary Florence Nightingale helped in the designs for the ward layout. This enabled the hospital to accommodate 2,000 in-patients and 3,000 out-patients yearly.

Of the new infirmary the *Yorkshire Post* wrote in 1866:

> *We shall not only have an infirmary sufficient for the wants of our ever-increasing population, but every internal arrangement will be perfect of its kind, while the building, taken as a whole, will be a model of architectural simplicity and propriety.*

The introduction of Listers antiseptic treatment came in 1864 at roughly the same time that the Leeds Infirmary was moved from Infirmary Street and the hospital was one of the first such institutions in the country to establish the success of the treatment which had originated in Edinburgh. Mr Pridgin Teale was the senior consulting

The second Infirmary, built in the 1700s. Thoresby Society

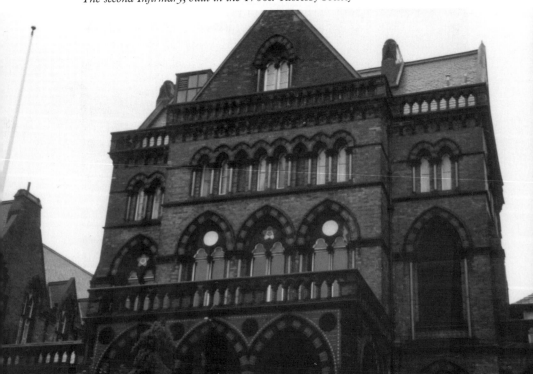

surgeon at the infirmary and saw the treatment become a common part of hospital procedure.

He saw how, through its operation, hundreds of thousands of lives were saved in the First World War. He said that more men died of disease in the Crimean War than had been killed in battle and he witnessed how the prevalence of hospital gangrene and erysipelas were counteracted and to a large extent eradicated by the antiseptic treatment.

In the absence of any national health provision, the hospitals were entirely dependent upon the city council and voluntary contributions. All proceeds from the annual carnival were given to the Workpeople's Hospital Fund and the Yorkshire Ladies Council was founded around 1870 as a charitable organisation to help young women to obtain education and training to widen their opportunities in work and everyday life. One aspect of the Council's work was in 'sanitary science'.

By the turn of the century more attention was being paid to the prevention of disease and hospitals were becoming more closely linked with charities. Work in the early part of the twentieth century was carried out for the benefit of out-patients by the lady almoners who had some medical training and acted as the allies of doctors. It was often found that people attending the hospital were really suffering from insufficient food or they had a condition directly related to the poor conditions at home. In such cases medicine was of little use and doctors were unable to help.

Such cases could be resolved by a special diet or a spell of residence in the clearer air of the countryside or by the sea. These cases were given to the almoner who had a room in the hospital and though she had no funds at her disposal, she was in close touch with the charities in Leeds and could often find some solution to the problem.

There were many cases where not one individual charity could provide all the help that a person needed, so the Charity Organisation Society which had five offices in Leeds undertook the work of bringing societies and charities together.

The society was in close touch with all the charitable societies in Leeds as well as institutions in other parts of the country which could have been useful to Leeds people. There were several charities for children in the town including the Invalid Children's Aid Society which had workshops for children with disabilities. There were also many workers who visited sick children in their homes.

The Leeds Children's Relief Fund began in 1904 with five dinners given to the needy each week excluding Saturday and Sunday with the price set at a penny a head. The food was provided by the Leeds Children's Dinner Society, with typical meals consisting of ox head soup and bread, lentil soup and bread, Irish stew and rolled puddings.

There was concern that physical education should be an important aspect of any universal system of education, but it was almost absent from Leeds schools. Voluntary agencies such as boys clubs and scouts met the demand to some extent, but there were repeated calls for more time to be given to physical education in schools as was the case in the public schools of the day.

Though the conditions of many people had improved by the time Britain entered the twentieth century, Leeds was not immune from disease. As Britain attempted to return to as normal life as possible after the Great War of 1914–18 the country was hit by a particularly nasty outbreak of influenza. It reached Leeds in the October of 1918 and within eight days of the first signs appearing at Whingate Elementary School, half of its 400 pupils were absent. The Education Committee took the decision to close down schools in Leeds two days before the regular half-term break and pupils did not return to their classes until two and a half weeks had passed. About 150,000 people throughout Britain succumbed to the disease during the winter of 1918–19.

Leeds Union Workhouse, now the Thackray Medical Museum. The author

In the twentieth century the greatest change to public health was the establishment of the National Health Service after the Labour Government came to power in 1945 with existing hospitals in the city becoming part of the service. These included St James's Hospital which began life as the Workhouse Infirmary and culminated in it becoming one of the biggest hospitals in the country. The workhouse itself eventually became the Thackray Medical Museum.

6   *E*DUCATION

Education for children in Leeds dates back as far as 1341 with an informal teaching network having been established. However, formal education began in earnest when a priest called Sir William Sheafield formed Leeds Grammar School in 1552.

Sheafield had a commitment to providing education for the young and even included it in his will which read:

> *To the use and for findinge, sustination and liveinge of one honest substantial learned man to be schoole maister to teach and instruct freely forever. Younge schollars, youthes and children. That shall come and resort to him from time to time to be taught, instructed and informed in such a schoolhouse as shall be founded, erected and buylded by the paryshioners of the said towne and parishe of Leedes.*

The school was originally situated in a chantry chapel on Leeds Bridge but was moved in 1624 by John Harrison, the great benefactor, to North Street where it stood on a site between the present Grand Theatre and Vicar Lane, which was then the main road to Harrogate on the outskirts of town.

In reality, the school was just one large room, but Ralph Thoresby the famous Leeds historian wrote:

> *The school house was made in all respects sufficiently handsome and convenient according to the fashions of the times, which included not however the comforts of a fireplace or of a boarded floor.*

In 1691 Godfrey Lawson, who had been the mayor of Leeds two years previously received permission from fellow trustees to add a library to the school which was built a year later.

John Harrison, the great Leeds benefactor. Thoresby Society

Sport was an important part of the life of the school and though no proper football or cricket was practicable as the playground of the Harrison building was very small, cricket was played when the school moved to Woodhouse Moor in 1858. The school was then able to make full use of the open spaces and green fields which had previously been in short supply. By 1884 football was being played on a field at the junction of Cardigan and Brudenell Road and cross-country runs were also favoured, by the school-masters if not the pupils! Traditionally the runs began in Meanwood.

In 1677 a new grammar school was built in Wortley and a number of new schools were opened in the Leeds area during the early years of the eighteenth century. There were now two grammar schools but at this time areas including Holbeck, Beeston, Chapeltown and Woodhouse were all able to provide some form of education for their children.

The Blue Coat School, a charity school, was opened in Leeds in 1705. Aiming to provide a level of education for some of the poorer children in the town, it was specifically aimed at preparing them for work and they were expected to be engaged in some sort of practical work on three afternoons a week. However, for most poorer children, their first form of education came in 1784 when the first Sunday school opened in Leeds.

Leeds Charity School. The author

Later in the century a School of Industry was formed in Beezon's Yard near Briggate which prepared women for domestic service.

The middle classes were much more fortunate in terms of their education and private education was already prevalent in the eighteenth century with such places as Mr Mills' writing school and Elizabeth Caulston's boarding school for young ladies.

By the beginning of the nineteenth century there were more people prepared to admit that education was important and was the key to providing a better society. Joseph Lancaster, who was an authority on the monotorial form of teaching spoke to people in the Music Hall in Leeds in 1809 and was to claim that one teacher assisted by older pupils who were to act as monitors could teach up to 1,000 children. His methods caught on and two years later a Lancasterian school for boys was formed in Leeds with one for girls established later.

In 1813 the Church of England opened a mixed National School off Kirkgate and with Sunday schools and dame schools now well established, there was more access to education for the children of the town.

The different denominations were effective in providing schooling whilst there were also as many as sixty evening schools to complement them. Free schooling was also now available for some of those who could not pay, with two ragged schools; two industrial schools and others attached to the Leeds and Hunslet workhouses.

In 1822, John Marshall, who helped develop flax-spinning machinery for the booming woollen trade in the 1790s, persuaded the owners of several other firms in Holbeck to join him in establishing a school in the area.

So, in May 1825, Marshall began sending children from his mills to a day school. At first he selected thirty children aged between eleven and twelve, who he believed would most benefit from schooling, but the number soon grew to sixty and fifty more of the older children were educated free every Monday evening.

John Marshall. Thoresby Society

Overseers were instructed to send only those who were 'well-behaved and wanted to go'. The children were taught to read and write and the girls were also taught some household skills including sewing while the boys were taught a course in accounting.

Marshall was a prolific figure in the town at this time. He was involved in the founding of a Mechanics' Institute and a Literary and Philosophical Society in Leeds and in 1826 he began a campaign to establish a university in the town. Marshall gave money to the Leeds Library and with Peter Garforth and a small group of Unitarians, helped to re-establish the *Leeds Mercury* under the editorship of Edward Baines.

In 1843 Marshall gave an insight into life inside the school. He said that the school was part of the factory, though it was open to all the children who lived in the neighbourhood 'whose parents choose to adopt the regulations laid down for its good governance'. He said:

The schoolrooms are comfortably warmed by hot-water apparatus; and there is a large plot of ground outside the building which serves as a playground. As to the internal discipline of the schools, there is the same busy hum, the same thumbing of slates, pencils and books, the same mixture of the slow-moving with the quick-moving intellect of the meek and placid boy while the young rogue who looks as if he loved marbles better than books, as in most schools.

The boys mostly wear a kind of short pinafore made of coarse flaxen cloth, called a 'harding' or 'harden'; and their appearance on the whole is certainly indicative of good health and high animal spirits.

Though there was some education for children in Leeds before 1870, it was inconsistent and there was no uniformity in terms of teaching. Each schoolmaster had the power to give his own interpretation on what the school lesson should consist of. Parents of middle class children could suggest to a school master the type of learning they desired for their child and if they considered that the child needed time to digest some part of the learning, they had the right to keep the child away from school for a day, week or even longer.

By 1817 the churches and chapels of Leeds catered for about 5,000 pupils and Sunday schools increased in popularity so that 130 existed in 1858 with about 35,000 children taking advantage of the resources. By the latter years of the nineteenth century Leeds had good day schools as well as mechanics institutes.

However, it was still largely the middle classes who were sending their children to school and there were many young children roaming

Leeds School Board. Formed following the Education Act of 1870. The author

the streets still unable to read or write. James Hole, the social reformer said that in Leeds, 'large masses are yet steeped in the grossest ignorance'. Many people in Leeds and beyond began to feel that education was too important an issue to be left almost solely to the religious bodies of the time.

Central Higher Grade School. The author

It was felt that state involvement was essential to prepare children more fully for the newly industrialised world that awaited them. Therefore, in 1870, the Education Act was passed which led to the formation of school boards and eventually compulsory, free, education.

As a consequence of the act, in November 1870, the first Leeds school board was elected to office with Sir Andrew Fairbairn voted in as chairman. The board got to work quickly establishing thirteen schools in premises such as public halls. The first purpose-built school was at Bewerley Street opening in 1873 and also that year, four evening schools were provided along with specialist arts and science classes.

By 1882 the board was further advanced in establishing education for all and it decided to cater more fully for the brighter pupils in the town. Seen initially as a challenge to the Grammar School and the Leeds Church Middle Class School, the Central Higher Grade School nevertheless opened for boys and girls in 1885, moving to Woodhouse Lane in 1889. By the 1880s the school board had erected forty new schools and by the turn of the century this had grown to about eighty, both secondary and elementary.

In 1874 the Yorkshire College of Science opened its doors on Cookbridge Street with the aim of encouraging more adults into education. Specialising in science and the arts it was also strongly focused on manufacturing, mining, engineering and agriculture which were all well established industries in the Yorkshire area. By 1877 the college had moved, with financial support, into its present building at the university off Woodhouse Lane.

Also, the Leeds Girls' Grammar School Company began in 1875, changing its name to the Leeds Girls' High School Company Limited. In 1866 it opened a school at St James's Lodge, Woodhouse Lane but by 1907 the decision was made to move the school and it settled into its current location.

The Education Act of 1870 had revolutionised education in the Leeds area, however, there were many changes still to be made and in November 1895 the Report of the Royal Commission into Secondary Education was published. Set up to look into the best way to establish a well-organised system for secondary education in the country, the report stated that:

Not a few censuses have dilated upon the disadvantages from which young Englishmen suffer in industry and commerce owing to the superior preparation of their competitors in several countries in Continental Europe. These disadvantages are real but we attach no less importance to the thoughts of dullness and barrenness to which so many lived are condemned.

At the absence of those capacities for intellectual enjoyment which ought to be awakened in youth. In an age of increasing leisure and luxury when men have more time and opportunity for pleasure and pursue it more eagerly, it comes all the more desirable that they should induced to draw it from the best sources.

Thus it is not merely in the interests of the material prosperity of intellectual activity of the nation but no less its happiness and its moral strength. The extension and reorganisation of secondary education seem entitled to a place among the first subjects with which social legislation ought to deal.

Following on from this, in 1911, the Leeds Education Secretary James Graham prepared a memorandum stating the reasons why he thought there should be a reconsideration of the school leaving age in Leeds. He said that the industrial circumstances of the city had led to a considerable number of boys over the age of fourteen who were out of work. The situation at that time had meant that younger boys were replacing boys of fifteen or over.

He added that the unemployment of boys aged fourteen and fifteen was not due to laziness and that if the labour market was reorganised it would be possible to raise the school age and yet have exactly the same amount of work being done and the same amount of wages earnt by the boy population under the age of twenty.

Graham's plans were popular and in 1918 an education act raised the school-leaving age to fourteen and meant that for the first time young children could not work in factories, mines or workshops.

Leeds University

Leeds University first became a thought on 14 January 1826 when an article appeared in the *Leeds Mercury* regarding a scheme for the establishment of a university in Leeds. John Marshall, who had been such an important figure in the education life of the town, was the President of the Philosophical and Literary Society at the time and wrote a paper on the present situation of education in England. He considered it a vital preparation for active life.

Later a Member of Parliament for Yorkshire, Marshall initially proposed that the whole circle of literature, science and the arts would be offered to students attending university. He was also keen to see that there should be no bar as to the admission of students and that it would embrace the education of boys from a young age to the age when they entered mercantile life, usually between sixteen and eighteen.

However, the idea for a university in Leeds did not reappear until later in the nineteenth century, when it grew out of the Yorkshire

Leeds University Parkinson Building. The author

College of Science, which was founded in 1874. The oldest branch of the university is the Leeds School of Medicine, founded in 1831. This became incorporated into Yorkshire College as its department of medicine in 1884 and in 1904 the University of Leeds received its charter.

School life

With education beginning to attain greater importance in society, thoughts were turned onto how to teach the children. Equipment at first was primitive and school lessons would look very different to how they are today. Pupils learnt letters and numbers using sand trays, wooden trays with a sprinkling of sand, with which they traced the letters and the figures. Occasionally they used slates.

School games included pye's ball which was essentially rounders, whilst skipping and racing were also popular.

For those children who did not behave, there were some schools which used the cane whilst others administered punishments by a slap on the back of the hand with a ruler or a teacher's hand. Other punishments, included pupils having to put their hands on their heads, to stand in the corner or to stand on a seat in the classroom.

Sunday school began in the morning at nine, and in the afternoon at one, going on until four o'clock and its influence was commonly seen, especially in the factories where it manifested itself through the singing of the workers and the fact that the more thoughtful and intelligent workers would often have a book to hand, more often than not a well-thumbed bible or testament.

Education was not distributed equally to boys and girls. Women were taught at school largely to equip themselves for a life at home as a housewife. Quarry Mount council school for example saw its purpose as making clear to mothers that their daughters attending the elementary schools in the city, knew how to sew and darn, cut out simple garments, bake bread and pastry and prepare cheap and wholesome dinners.

When cooking was first introduced into the elementary schools, some mothers protested, seemingly annoyed that the school authorities were doing a job they were intending to do themselves. Mothers regarded it as their duty to teach their daughters to cook in as much the same way as it was their duty to teach them to walk and talk. However, some others appeared to welcome the intervention of the schools and one newspaper complained of some mothers:

Now they go to the other extreme and they are inclined to leave everything to the school-mistress and many of the children do not get the chances for cooking and sewing at home that they deserve.

For those who lived in poverty in Leeds, and there were many, the Leeds Holiday School was founded to provide, for the very poorest children in Leeds elementary schools, the chance of a good time during the vacation. A Leeds newspaper article commented on the scheme:

For such children the courts and alleys are their only playground out of school hours and they wander aimlessly around the streets and roads ready for mischief. At the best they are doing themselves no good in any way. They do not even know how to play games.

Among the activities on offer at the holiday school was a course in gymnastics while girls were given dolls to dress and boys were given the opportunity of 'making things' such as toy boats out of blocks of wood. The girls also made bread, cakes and buns which they were allowed to eat afterwards.

In the afternoon at the holiday school, some of the boys were able to play cricket in the East End Park whilst the girls visited the Girls' High School in Headingley. The report adds:

It is a joyous fact that at first the children would not drink milk nor eat plain, wholesome food provided for them. They had no appetite for it. Probably the highly seasoned 'delicacies' of the slums had spoilt them. At any rate, not the least useful of the lessons they have learnt is to eat and enjoy plain, wholesome fare, and they are much better for it.

From the mid-eighteenth century there were always some of the middle classes who were eager to further their education. These were the people responsible for the first library in the town which opened in 1768 when the Leeds Library occupied the ground floor of the Rotation Office in Kirkgate. A new subscription library was opened in Albion Street in 1793, mainly for those who came out of the Leeds Library membership.

The Central Lending library in Leeds dates back to 1871, when it was based in the building once occupied by the old Leeds Infirmary on Infirmary Street.

Throughout the latter part of the nineteenth century the council began to introduce libraries to the population. A librarian was appointed to Leeds in 1870, the same year that saw branch libraries open in Holbeck and Hunslet. Purpose-built libraries began to be built in the town but before this temporary libraries were set up in schools and even in a police station.

7 ℱRADE AND INDUSTRY

B y 1207, when the Lord of the Manor, Maurice De Gant, founded a new town at Leeds, trade and commerce were increasing in England and many new towns were seen on the landscape. De Gant created a new street of houses west of the existing village and divided the land into plots for building whilst craftsmen built houses and paid rent to the Lord for the land. A charter was then granted which enabled people to live at a fixed rent to hold their own court and practice commerce and craftsmanship.

The new street was thought to have been called Bridge Gata, *gata* being an old word for street, and in time it was changed to Briggate. The little village consisted of butchers, bakers, carpenters and blacksmiths although the principal industry, even then was the manufacture of wool.

By the middle ages, Leeds was still a small village, concentrated around the Parish Church, but it did hold a weekly market and there were also two fairs held which attracted people from all over Yorkshire to trade.

Though the woollen trade was the main industry in Leeds, the village was surrounded by countryside where agriculture was the staple industry. For many it was merely a way of providing themselves with the necessary food for their family. A seventeenth century inventory showed that only a small percentage of farmers had more than six cows, as most families kept a few in order to keep themselves provided with milk, cheese and butter. However, by the first quarter of the eighteenth century more farmers were turning to dairying as a way of selling products to expanding local markets in Leeds, Otley and Wetherby.

Crops cultivated at this time included corn, wheat, oats, barley, rye, mazelin, peas and beans. Rape was sown by many as it was a good crop for fattening sheep and for centuries the only form of sweetening for food was honey, so many people kept bees, a practice which continued into the eighteenth century.

By the nineteenth century the growing of turnips for winter fodder was slowly becoming established. Potatoes would be used mainly as cattle-feed, and oats by far the largest crop, pointed to the staple diet of northern folk at this time. Oatmeal supplied them with breakfast and supper and oatcakes, baked on an iron griddle, were a popular dish.

The 1840s saw another surge in agricultural development in Yorkshire as farmers began supplying the rapidly expanding Victorian towns of the West Riding with wheat, beef, mutton and milk. New fertilisers were purchased; new machinery aided the farmers' cause and the developing railway system pointed to a better transport system.

Farming became more specialised and scientific as the nineteenth century developed. Institutions grew around the trade such as the Yorkshire Agricultural Society in 1837 and the Royal Agricultural Society a year later. Both of these organisations had many Yorkshire tenants and landowners as members in an era which became known as 'high farming'.

In spite of improved transport techniques and better transport, the golden age of farming did not last and from 1875 to 1880 several seasons of cold, wet weather meant that the resulting crops were poor. This occurred at a time when cheap imports of wheat and other crops were being flown into the country from across the Atlantic assisted by fast steamships, railways and the advent of refrigeration. Prices in Britain came tumbling down, as local farmers could not compete, culminating in a significant agricultural depression.

This situation was exacerbated by the Industrial Revolution which led to there being plenty of work available in the woollen towns. People who had previously been farm workers in the agricultural districts of Yorkshire flocked into town in order to find work. At the same time the production of cloth in the remote Dales areas was destroyed by the rapid growth of the urban woollen industry. Lead mining and quarrying also declined and for the workers in rural areas often the only alternative to upping sticks and migrating into Leeds was to concentrate on now limited agricultural activities and associated crafts. Numbers employed in agriculture steadily declined throughout the nineteenth century, especially after 1851.

Up until the early part of the fourteenth century, cloth was not made very successfully in England, but in 1336 Edward III encouraged its manufacture and a large number of flanders weavers settled in the north of England, helping the production of cloth in towns such as Halifax, York and Leeds. Fulling mills were strategically placed alongside minor streams and the corn mills would have grown in proportion to the town's needs. To prevent foreign competition the export of cloth was forbidden.

The Woollen Industry became more firmly established in the Middle Ages using home-grown wool. Production was based on the domestic system and Leeds became a market centre where the cloth

The Calls. A historical part of Leeds in its own right, was where the Fletland Mills was situated. The Mills produced a large amount of corn for the Leeds district. The author

was exchanged and finished. The output of broadcloth in the area rose from 30,000 pieces in the late 1720s to 60,000 pieces in the 1740s.

Leeds and villages in the surrounding countryside to the west specialised in the making of 'Northern Dozens' or 'Yorkshire Broadcloths' – cheap good quality cloths which spurred on the growth of Leeds and the West Riding in general throughout the late sixteenth and early seventeenth century.

A strategically located town with a market was needed for this trade, to supply the raw materials, to supply a market for the product, to organise the sale and export of the product and to supply a food market for the workers.

For a time Halifax and Wakefield may have been possible candidates to fulfil this role but Leeds had overtaken them in size and importance by the 1660s. Leeds' situation was ideal – situated at an important bridging point on the River Aire with links to the sea via the River Humber to the east and links to the wool and cloth producing districts of moorland Calderdale and Airedale to the west.

It was also situated on the edge of the rich agricultural Vale of York from which supplies of food could be brought in for the cloth workers to buy.

At this time Leeds was still a relatively small town, hardly longer than the length of Briggate and stretching westwards no further than Trinity church. The entire town was situated on the northern side of the River Aire and the old Norman bridge at the foot of Briggate was still sufficient for the weekly market.

As towns such as Halifax and Wakefield were well-placed geographically to benefit from the growth of the cloth trade, Leeds kept hold of its position as the dominant town by holding a Monday market when people from all over Yorkshire braved the poor road conditions to buy and sell their goods. The traders of the town and the country manufacturers were called together by a bell rung in the Bridge Chapel. The merchants of Hull, Boston and other towns came to Leeds to buy and carry down their cloth, often transporting it by river.

The market, which took place on the bridge spanning the River Aire, on the site of the present Leeds Bridge, was held as early as 1488.

Most of the wool was made into cloth by small manufacturers scattered around the country. These manufacturers bought or sent their goods to the markets of Leeds, Bradford and Wakefield. During the time of Benjamin Gott, wool and worsted was worked exclusively by hand; the wool was first sorted then carded by the manual labour of men and boys before being spun, usually by women and then finally submitted to the handloom weaver.

Leeds continued to flourish during the seventeenth century as a market town and as the town where broad cloths were expertly finished by dressers, croppers and dyers. In the West Yorkshire towns, men sometimes worked full-time as clothiers for a few large scale employers and in 1629 Leeds manufacturers were said to be daily employing about forty people.

As trade increased a second market was held on Saturdays, so Leeds now held two markets a week until it was decided that due to the increase in trade, the market had become too big for its site and was an inconvenience to other bridge users. In 1684 the Mayor of Leeds decided that the market had to move and it became established in High Street, now known as Lower Briggate.

At the beginning of the eighteenth century, Leeds suffered a threat to its position when Wakefield, another strong cloth town in Yorkshire tried to entice those clothiers who travelled to the Leeds market by

White Cloth Hall. Clothiers met here twice a week to trade in undyed 'white' woollen cloth. The author

opening its own cloth hall. The Wakefield merchants believed that their offer of an enclosed hall would be more attractive to those currently having to brave the elements of the outside market in Leeds.

However, Leeds responded to this threat by opening the White Cloth Hall in Kirkgate in 1711. This was only for undyed cloths and the market for coloured cloth continued to be held in Lower Briggate. However, this trade also increased and it was necessary to move premises to a less congested site, also on Briggate, before, eventually, another coloured cloth hall, was soon built, this time near Mill Hill. A third cloth hall, capable of holding over 1,000 stalls was built in Call Lane in 1775 in a bid to cater for the burgeoning demand.

In 1724 Daniel Defoe visited Leeds and described the town's cloth market as 'a prodigy of its kind unequalled in the world'. He described seeing the clothiers arriving early in the morning and 'as few Clothiers bring more than one piece, the market being so frequent, they go into the inns and public houses with it, and there set it down'. He went into more detail, saying:

Cloth Hall Court, the site of the Coloured Cloth Hall. The author

> *At about 6 o'clock in the morning and 7 in winter the market bell at the old chapel by the bridge rings and soon the whole market filled and all the trestles filled with cloth. At about half an hour after eight o'clock the market bell again rings upon which the buyers disappear. The cloth is all sold or, if any remain, it is carried back to the inns.*

The invention of an efficient flax-spinning machine by John Marshall and Matthew Murray which produced good quality yarn and the building of Temple Mill at Water Lane helped the growth of the textile industry in Leeds. The introduction of steam-powered machinery in the late eighteenth century also encouraged the building of textile factories in the town. Farming land, north-east and south of the town, was purchased and filled with rows of back-to-back terraced

Bank Mills, the waterside flax mill built in 1831. The author

houses to accommodate the local workers. Houses were also built by filling in the long, narrow crofts behind the streets of houses, shops and inns of Leeds. In 1801 Leeds had a population of 30,669, but by 1831 it had more than doubled to reach 67,554.

The textile trade continued to flourish and the numerous coal mines in the area provided fuel for the increasing population and for the textile factories which continued to emerge. By 1855 Leeds had thirty-seven flax mills, which employed nearly 10,000 people, mainly women, children and Irish immigrants. Leeds also had a flourishing trade in carpets, cotton, yarn and silk. The textile trade provided an important market for the machines and steam engines which were produced in local engineering works. Predominant among the local entrepreneurs who led the way were Benjamin Gott and John Marshall.

The woollen cloth manufacturer Gott became one of Europe's largest employers. His Bean Ing Mill which opened on a sixteen-acre site in 1792 was the largest woollen factory in Leeds and was the first to concentrate all the processes of manufacture under one roof. His smaller mill at Armley is now the Leeds Industrial Museum.

John Marshall was eighteen when Kendrew and Porthouse produced a flax-spinning machine and he produced a good deal of energy and money in trying to improve the process and also make serviceable the other instruments necessary for the production of linen.

The rapid growth of linen production in the town led to increased trade between Leeds and other parts of the country and with foreign markets. It also encouraged manufacturers to settle in Leeds.

Leeds position as the main market for the trade in woollen goods was helped in the eighteenth century by the building of the 127-mile long Leeds & Liverpool Canal and the Aire & Calder Navigation which linked Leeds with Hull and the River Humber. Leeds also had the advantage of having the oldest horse-drawn railroad in the world. Built in 1758, this four-mile railroad supplied the people of Leeds with coal from the Middleton Colliery.

The economic importance of Leeds was increased in 1840 with the completion of the Manchester & Leeds Railway. This line was, in 1847 to

Benjamin Gott. Thoresby Society

become the principal constituent of the Lancashire and Yorkshire Railway. Leeds was now linked to Liverpool on the west coast and Goole and Hull to the east. The population of Leeds grew rapidly after the development of the railway network and by 1861 the town had a population of 207,000, making Leeds comfortably the largest town in Yorkshire.

With the railway boom it soon became apparent to those with warehouses that proximity to the new stations was increasingly desirable. Buyers who came into Leeds from different towns in the north usually travelled by train and were unwilling to stray far from the station when they arrived. Time was precious and so the larger merchants and manufacturers left their warehouses in distant parts of the town and built themselves new ones before, soon, the whole of the area around Wellington Street was transformed into large blocks of warehouses.

By the Victorian Age Britain had emerged as a major industrial nation and could claim to be the 'workshop of the world'. Leeds was part of that success as it saw new industries begin to make their

St Paul's House was originally a warehouse and a cloth-cutting works. The author

impact upon the town. The woollen and flax industries were still active well into the twentieth century, but as the nineteenth century continued old industries, including engineering expanded and new industries such as ready-made clothing emerged. Leeds was fortunate in having a diversified industrial base and other dominant industries including leather, printing and brewing began to flourish.

By 1850 Leeds was a town of many diverse trades. At the beginning of the nineteenth century, it had overtaken Wakefield as the leading centre of leather production in West Yorkshire and by 1870, Leeds was also the leading centre for sheepskins as well as becoming a big producer of the tanning of hides.

Leeds also excelled in the pottery business and it became a trade known throughout the continent with lucrative markets, especially in

The Corn Exchange. The author

Russia and Norway. The main Leeds pottery was on an extensive site between Jack Lane and the old Wagon Road in Hunslet.

There was also a trade in the printing and publishing of books and music. Important editions of *The Pilgrim's Progress* and *Robinson Crusoe* were produced in Leeds. There was also a brickmaking industry and there were many craftsmen such as coachmakers, clockmakers, booksellers and jewellers established in the town as well as many other trades including butchers, bakers, barbers, innkeepers, carpenters, blacksmiths and glaziers.

Therefore, by 1900, Leeds boasted a varied economic base and alternative forms of employment were made available by its flourishing commercial activities. The ready-made clothing and textile industry, then pioneered by off-the-peg clothing manufacturers such

Oakwood Clock, centrepiece of the new Leeds market in 1904. The author

as Montague Burton, operated successfully alongside the printing and engineering industries. John Waddington became the world's biggest playing card and games manufacturer and Clarke, Fowler and Kitson ran the biggest engineering works in Yorkshire. As such, Leeds never experienced the mass depression suffered by many single-industry towns.

Meanwood Tannery, was one of the biggest tanneries in the country. The author

By the 1920s, the textile industry was declining, but other, related industries ensured that Leeds did not suffer as a city. Tailoring for a mass market flourished as did the leather industry and there were many boot and shoe makers. The Burton tailoring factory – the largest in Europe – employed 16,000 people at its peak in the mid-1920s.

Other notable figures in Leeds trade began to emerge, this time away from the woollen industry. Michael Marks was a man born in Russia but who moved to Leeds as a young man in the late 1800s. Unable to speak English, he joined a company called Barran that was known to employ Jewish refugees. In 1884 he secured a deal with a warehouse owner for him to buy goods and then sell them in the villages around Leeds. The venture was a success and Marks soon raised enough money to establish a stall in Leeds' open market.

He was also able to rent an area at the new covered market in Leeds, selling goods that only cost a penny. He promoted his stall with a big poster telling customers 'Don't Ask the Price, It's a Penny'. Over the next few years Marks opened similar penny stalls in covered market halls all over Yorkshire and Lancashire.

Leeds Pottery, the original building. The author

In 1894 Marks decided to expand his business and eventually met up with a man named Tom Spencer, who, seeing that Marks had set up a formidable business, saw the £300 investment asked for as worthwhile. History records that he was right!

By the 1700s Leeds had two thriving newspapers. John Hirst founded the *Leeds Mercury* in 1718 and the *Leeds Intelligencer* came along in 1754. The two papers, liberal and conservative respectively ran in fierce competition before other papers, notably the *Yorkshire Post* and the *Yorkshire Evening Post* followed towards the end of the nineteenth century.

Leeds was also well known for its brewing industry and by 1866 there were thirty-three breweries operating in the town. The most famous was undoubtedly Joshua Tetley & Son Ltd. The firm was borne out of the Tetley family taking over an existing brewing business run by William Sykes. William Tetley was described as a

The former premises of Charles Walker & Co, mill furnishers, an example of supplementary industries to the main textile trade. The author

'considerable maltster' based in Armley and up until 1822 the Tetley business was primarily as maltsters and wine and brandy merchants, trading as William Tetley and Sons.

In 1822 Tetley took over the brewery of William Sykes at Salem Place, a long established business dating back to 1796. Joshua Tetley took over the business on the death of William and was left to run the malting in Armley and the brewery in Leeds. In 1890 Joshua Tetley bought his first pub, the *Duke William* in Bowman Lane. The pub, now closed, remains within the brewery grounds.

Several new shopping arcades were built in Leeds as the nineteenth century drew to a close. Thornton's Arcade was built in 1878 and it was followed by Queens Arcade in 1889 and the Grand Arcade and Victoria Arcade in 1898.

By the early twentieth century the main industries were engineering, including the making of tram rails, and tailoring. During the century that followed, the importance of manufacturing industry declined whilst service industries grew rapidly. In 1951, fifty-five per cent of the workforce were employed in manufacturing but by 1973 it had fallen to less than thirty-five per cent. Many people worked in banking, insurance, pubs and hotels. The city council was itself a major employer. In 1946 it employed 19,000 people but thirty years later the figure had risen to 35,000.

8   *P*OLITICS

By the early part of the thirteenth century Leeds had attained some civic importance and its burgesses were granted a charter. However, the Norman Baron who had become lord of the manor had granted only a very limited degree of freedom to the citizens. Under the feudal system there was little room for the expansion of civic government though that changed once the system disappeared.

King Charles I granted the first charter of incorporation in 1626, under which the town elected a council consisting of one alderman and nine burgesses with twenty assistants. By 1661 a second charter was granted by King Charles II, which gave permission for Leeds to have a mayor, the first being Thomas Danby. The following year the borough was divided into six wards in order to improve distribution of relief for the poor.

In 1835 the municipals corporation act was passed and the old charters were superseded. The borough was divided; this time into twelve wards with sixteen aldermen and forty-eight councillors and in 1893 another important change saw a royal charter from Queen Victoria, which granted Leeds city status.

Adam Baynes became the first MP to represent Leeds when he won a seat at the elections of 1654. The town was represented due to a redistribution of seats from rotten and pocket boroughs. However, when Richard Cromwell became Prime Minister in 1658 the town lost its MP and was to remain unrepresented until the *Reform Bill* in 1832.

Politics during the eighteenth and nineteenth centuries was unrecognisable to what we see today. On Woodhouse Moor, at election time, what were known as the 'hustings' were erected on the lower part of the Moor. Instead of a cross by the side of the preferred candidate in a ballot box, the only franchise open to the voters was a show of hands and the making of as much noise as possible.

King Charles I. Royal.gov.uk

King Charles II. Royal.gov.uk

During the 1800s the larger towns were filling up rapidly with more people from agricultural districts coming into town to look for work. Leeds, Manchester and Birmingham were three of the biggest, yet they were not directly represented in Parliament while much smaller towns with just a few thousand inhabitants were able to send their Member of Parliament to sit in the Palace of Westminster.

Borough representation was bought as openly as eggs in a market and voting qualification was fixed at a high rental. Those who were entitled to vote had to go to York in order to carry out their wish though this was for county elections only.

Though Leeds did not have its own MPs during the eighteenth and early nineteenth century, the town nevertheless played an active role in the political process. In the elections of 1807 there were two Yorkshire seats. William Wilberforce was elected without opposition, however there was a contest for the second seat between the Whigs and the Tories. Lord Milton got into parliament for the Whigs by about a thousand votes, but it was a fierce contest and the two Leeds newspapers took opposing sides. The *Leeds Intelligencer* was strongly on the side of the Tories whilst the *Leeds Mercury* was usually on the side of the Whigs.

Issues on which the two papers were to vent their editorial spleen included the repeal of the Corn Laws, Catholic Emancipation and slavery, a topic on which William Wilberforce was to become especially concerned.

The *Reform Bill* in 1832 saw the political climate change and for the first time since Cromwell's parliament, Leeds was able to send members to London to represent the town. This increased the political hothouse atmosphere in the town generated by the two newspapers. At the General Election Edward Baines, owner of the *Leeds Mercury* supported the two Whig candidates, John Marshall, the owner of the largest flax-spinning factory in Leeds, and the historian Thomas Macaulay.

Voting for the 1832 election took place in the Cloth Hall yard, the scene of many political events and Marshall with 2,012 votes and Macaulay with 1,914 were elected MPs whilst Tory Michael Sadler, the leader of the factory reform movement received only 1,590 votes and was defeated. When Marshall came forth to address the voters in delivering his victory speech, a large poster was thrust before him and passed through the crowd showing his mill in a snowstorm with a large number of half-naked shivering children on their way to work in the mill.

The poster bore the words 'The scene in Water Lane at five o'clock in the morning'. Michael Thomas Sadler, the Tory candidate was a fierce opponent of child labour and he considered that Marshall's mill was a proponent of this practice. The poster infuriated the Liberal candidates and a rush was made for it. A fight ensued and proceedings at the count had to be halted until special constables were drafted in and divided the two camps.

In 1833 Macaulay resigned his seat in order to take up a post in India and Edward Baines was chosen as the Liberal candidate to replace him.

It was widely expected that Baines would take his political ambitions further and Westminster had long appeared to be his likely destination. He had bought the *Leeds Mercury* in 1801 and, as a political figure with strong views he was now able to use his paper to express them to the wider Leeds populace. Although in favour of some aspects of parliamentary reform, Baines disagreed with the working class being given the vote and his criticisms of those advocating universal suffrage resulted in him becoming very unpopular with radicals in Leeds.

In the election of February 1834 Edward Baines gained 1,951 votes and narrowly defeated the Tory candidate, Sir John Beckett who polled 1,917, resulting in Baines being elected as MP for Leeds. He was an active member of the House of Commons, supporting the cause of the Dissenters which included the measure to abolish Church Rates and the bill to register Dissenters' Marriages. He also played an important role in the opposition to factory legislation, universal suffrage and government control over education.

Edward Baines, MP and editor of the Leeds Mercury. Spartacus Educational

Declining health forced Baines to retire from the House of Commons in May 1841 and his suggestion that his friend, Joseph Hume, should replace him was accepted. However in the election that followed, William Beckett, the Tory candidate, defeated him.

Another important figure in the shaping of political Leeds was Samuel Smiles, who hailed from Edinburgh. It was during his time in the Scottish capital that he gained a deep interest in parliamentary reform. By 1837 Smiles had begun writing articles on parliamentary reform for the *Leeds Times* and the following year he became the

Temperance House and Mechanics' Institute, founded by Samuel Smiles. The author

newspaper's editor.

From this time on he devoted his life to the movement for political change. Through the pages of his newspaper he wrote on his hatred of the aristocracy and made attempts to unite working and middle class reformers. He also campaigned in favour of factory legislation.

In May 1840 Smiles became Secretary to the Leeds Parliamentary Reform Association, an organisation devoted to household suffrage, the secret ballot, equal representation, short parliaments and the abolition of the property qualification for parliamentary candidates. A decade later he was the founder of the Temperance Hall and Mechanics' Institute from where he and his friends gave lessons in reading and writing.

By this time the Chartist movement was at its peak though perhaps surprisingly, Smiles was not an enthusiastic supporter of the movement. He had become disillusioned with the movement's calls for physical force and began to stress the importance of 'individual reform' whilst promoting the idea of 'self-help'. His book *Self-Help*, which preached industry, thrift and self-improvement was published in 1859.

Chartism

Chartism was a different phenomenon in different parts of the country, so Leeds Chartism was different and distinct from Chartism in Lancashire. Yorkshire had a strong tradition of Tory radicalism with a belief in economic reform and Yorkshire also had more evidence of self-help movements and moderate, traditional radicalism with a strong connection between the workers, the Tory party and Tory Radicalism.

In the 1820s and 1830s, Leeds was a highly active centre for working-class radicalism and the Association of the Friends of Radical Reform was set up in Leeds in 1819. Radical literature and ideas flourished in the town and working men attended meetings calling for political reform.

In 1835 the Leeds Radical Association was formed and displayed a deep distrust of Whiggery, promoting a strong programme of equal representation, annual parliaments, universal suffrage, secret ballot and no property qualification for MPs. When the Six Points were adopted in 1838, they were familiar ideas to the Leeds radicals.

During the winter of 1837–38, the militants were strengthened due to the struggle against the new Poor Law in the West Riding, the trial of the Glasgow cotton spinners whose strike leaders were sentenced to transportation, the general trade depression and the *Northern Star* newspaper. The paper was important because it made the most powerful Chartist voice available to local Chartism, giving detailed reports of any radical meetings anywhere in Yorkshire and becoming an institution in working-class gatherings. It was widely read and public readings extended its audience considerably.

One such radical meeting was held on 15 October 1838 on Hartshead Moor. Set up like a fair there was food and drink available and many families attended. People came from Leeds, Bradford, Huddersfield and Halifax in their thousands, each group with its band playing and banners flying.

It was to be the first of many such gatherings and in the winter of 1838–39, vast torchlight meetings were held with speeches and schemes becoming more violent and inflammatory.

Universal suffrage was another cause which brought people together, again to demonstrate and one famous occasion was the West Riding Manhood Suffrage demonstration which took place on 8 October 1866. Many people gathered on Woodhouse Moor, some no doubt through curiosity, to witness the grand demonstration of which so much had been heard in the days preceding the event. From early morning the streets had been full of people making their way towards the Moor or the Town Hall from where the procession left.

Many people on the procession wore, on their hats or coats, tickets with the inscription 'Manhood suffrage and the ballot', which was the watchword of the reform league. Many shops were closed along the route of the procession and many tradesmen complained at the effect the march would have on their businesses. However landlords of the public houses were not amongst the complainants as all pubs along the route were full and had to lock their doors to prevent more coming in. All the windows which lined the route the march took were crowded long before the start.

Political demonstrations were ways of bringing the community together but borough and county elections during the nineteenth century also achieved this and they were always awaited with great anticipation with the mills stopping to give all hands an opportunity of attending nominations. On polling days for the county elections, many active voters used to meet to have breakfast together before a day of celebration would occur. Bands would start a procession with many on horseback and others in gigs and spring carts.

Following the bands would be other vehicles such as carrying carts, filled by voters who were ready to shout to the streets in favour of their particular party.

Other political gatherings saw great rejoicing over the repeal of the Corn Laws in 1846. There were celebrations in Pudsey and a giant plum pudding, boiled in a large dye-pan at one of the mills, was provided for those who had gathered. Afterwards, the pudding was hoisted onto a wherry and was paraded through the streets. In other places, oxen were roasted whole as were sheep.

Those who campaigned for the vote rejoiced when the 1867 Reform Act proposed by Benjamin Disraeli gave the vote to every male adult householder living in a borough constituency. Male lodgers paying £10 for unfurnished rooms were also granted the vote, leading to over a million men eligible to take part in the political process, though women would have longer to wait. The Reform Act also dealt with constituencies and boroughs with less than 10,000 inhabitants lost one of their MPs. The forty-five seats left available were distributed and extra ones were given to large towns including Liverpool, Manchester, Birmingham and Leeds.

The bill meant that another 30,000 Leeds voters were granted the vote and most of these were Liberal Party supporters, favouring the party which dominated both national and local politics during the greater part of the nineteenth century. It wasn't until November 1895 following the Conservative Party's landslide election victory that the party gained a foothold on the council in Leeds.

Elections in the late 1800s saw William Gladstone elected to represent Leeds in the 1880 general election, however he was also elected to a Scottish seat and, faced with the choice, he went up north. In the following Leeds by-election, his son Herbert was returned unopposed. A year later William, as Prime Minister, visited Leeds as a way of saying thank you for having elected him.

With the future of Ireland, a major issue of concern, not least to the many Irish immigrants who had settled in Leeds, Prime Minister Gladstone addressed the topic in the Cloth Hall, making a speech saying that 'the resources of civilisation are not exhausted'.

After the Cloth Hall meeting there was a torchlight procession and between 250,000 and 300,000 paraded through the streets of the city in his honour. Students from the Yorkshire College dragged a carriage containing Gladstone to the home of Sir James Kitson MP. The next day, Charles Stewart Parnell, the leader of the Irish home rulers group was arrested and detained in prison.

The Irish issue was an important one in the general election of 1885. That year the redistribution act had divided Leeds into five constituencies; central, north, south, west and east. Two days before the polls opened, Parnell issued a manifesto calling for all Irishmen with the vote to use it to oust Gladstone's Liberal's from power. The Irish in working class East Leeds did just that and the Conservative Dawson was elected as MP.

The Liberal Party nationally was also defeated and later that year Gladstone reverted to support for home rule. Parnell switched his vote to the Liberals and in the general election of the following year, the only Leeds seat to change hands was in the East Leeds constituency where Irish support for the Liberal Party saw them back in.

The Liberal Party was facing a fight to retain its dominance nationally, but it still had control of Leeds and this was the situation going into the election of 1895. In Leeds, municipal government had always been conducted on party

Prime Minister William Gladstone, a short-lived MP for Leeds. Spartacus Educational

lines and for sixty years the Liberals had a majority in the council chamber and monopolised the seats on the aldermanic bench and the office of chief magistrate. During the Liberals time in office they saw the city transformed with many public works. The Town Hall was erected as were the city library and art gallery.

However, they did not have one influential local newspaper on their side and the *Yorkshire Post* made its position clear in the run up to the election:

> *Dear electors of Leeds I have today to pronounce judgement on the great issue of whether the city is to remain subject to the Aldermanic Yoke under which it has so long and so helplessly groaned, or whether it is to witness the dawn of a brighter municipal era. The public have no love for the system to which the city has for so long misgoverned but if an end is to be made of it there must be a determination on the part of every voter to take the trouble to go to the poll.*

The paper went further in its championing of the Conservative cause, giving a list of the Tory candidates standing in the various wards and urging every voter to vote for them.

The Conservatives, strengthened by the Liberal Unionist Party, had gradually strengthened their position in the council, advocating a more aggressive policy and they finally took control of the council in the 1895 elections.

The Conservatives gained sixty seats, the Radicals thirty-seven, the Independents five and the Independent Labour Party picked up two seats with the Conservatives seeing big gains in the Leeds area. For the first time in the municipal history of the city the control of affairs had passed into Conservative hands, an event seen by the local papers as the most momentous election to have occurred in Leeds for some sixty years.

The Leeds and County Conservative Club was packed with supporters and Unionist workers throughout the night awaiting the results of the counting which took place at the Town Hall. One declaration after another was relayed to the club by telephone and messengers and when it became known, at about ten o'clock, that there had been a net Conservative gain there was a great outburst of cheering.

The atmosphere was naturally very different at the Liberal Club in Quebec Street when the results of the election became known. People assembled in the smoke room of the club and they soon became dejected when the first of the results came in.

However the two-party political scene which Leeds and the rest of the country had become used to, was soon about to change. Towards the end of the nineteenth century the political system, which had survived throughout Victoria's reign began to collapse.

There was beginning to be a groundswell of opinion in Leeds in favour of the emerging Labour movement within the country and in the autumn of 1887 Tom Maguire wrote a handbill in which he claimed that definite steps were taking place to create a Socialist Labour Party in Leeds.

Tom Maguire was one of the first men to become closely identified with the Labour movement in Leeds and became known for his assertion that the working men, whatever their political and religious views, were socially as one.

He became the secretary of the Socialist Democratic Federation which was founded in September 1884 and which later became the Socialist League. The League itself shut its doors in 1890 but the die was cast and the Labour movement soon became a major threat to both the Liberal Party and the Conservatives. With unemployment rising and those in work calling for better pay and improved working conditions the trade union movement gained lots of recruits. The city's manual workers were ideal for the burgeoning labour movement and in 1892 the Leeds Independent Labour Party was formed.

This was a year before Keir Hardie formed the national Labour Party, but the Leeds party was marginalised within the city at large due to its refusal to co-operate with the Leeds Trades and Labour Council.

By February 1900 the Labour Representative Committee, which eventually became the Labour Party, was formed. The movement was based on reform and socialism and it was aimed primarily at breaking the dominance of the Liberals in the city. However, many of the working classes were still supporters of the Liberals and in parliamentary elections the Liberal Party consistently held onto South Leeds. In West Leeds Labour did not even put up a candidate until 1914.

The picture was different in East Leeds which perhaps saw an early indication of tactical voting. In the general election of 1906, the Liberals did not put forward a candidate in the hope that the Labour Party's James O'Grady would defeat the Conservatives. It worked and he was to hold the seat until 1924.

Meanwhile, the struggle for women to get the vote intensified in the early part of the twentieth century and the Leeds Women's Suffrage Society became a well-known organisation in the city with Suffragette meetings often attracting crowds of over 100,000.

Isabella Ford was one of the movement's primary campaigners. Born in Leeds in 1855, she was raised in a political household with both her parents passionately interested in feminism, well before it became a popular campaigning issue. As a young woman, Isabella Ford met prominent feminists such as Josephine Butler and Elizabeth Garrett Anderson.

By the time Ford had reached the age of twenty, she was well versed in socialist principles and in 1883 she joined the Fabian Society. Two years later she helped Emma Patterson, President of the

Isabella Ford, prominent campaigner for women's rights in Leeds. Spartacus Educational

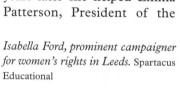

Women's Protective and Provident League, to form a Machinists' Society for tailoresses in Leeds. This was the start of a long campaign by Ford to improve the pay and conditions of women working in the textile industry in Leeds. In 1889 she established the Leeds Tailoresses' Union and the following year she was elected president of the organisation.

Ford retained her interest in women's rights and in 1890 she helped form the Leeds Women's Suffrage Society with her sister Bessie and sister-in-law, Helen Cordelia. Three years later, she was involved in forming a Leeds branch of the Independent Labour Party (ILP).

A friend of Isabella's was Mary Gawthorpe, also a strong supporter of women's rights and the two were instrumental in the setting up of the National Union of Women's Suffrage Societies. However Gawthorpe, though she began in Leeds Labour groups became disillusioned with the party, in particular its failure to act on the votes for women issue.

Gawthorpe joined the Woman's Social and Political Union and became a full-time organiser of the group in Leeds. The union was in favour of direct action and she famously heckled a speech given by Winston Churchill in 1909 and was badly beaten by stewards at the meeting, suffering severe internal injuries. She was also imprisoned

The grave of Isabella Ford. The author

several times while working for the WSPU. Hunger strikes and force-feeding badly damaged her health and in 1912 she had to abandon her active involvement in the movement.

Much has changed since the days of the suffragettes and Yorkshire has several women MPs, though Leeds itself is not well represented in this manner. However, through the years there have been many parliamentarians who have served the city well including Sir Keith Joseph, Hugh Gaitskell and Denis Healey.

Leeds Town Hall, from an Edwardian picture postcard c. 1909. Brian Elliott collection

9 *C*ULTURE

In pre-industrial times the cultural life of the town was predominately of a rural nature and was heavily determined by the seasons of the year. Therefore religious festivals were important and animals were often involved in other attractions with bull-baiting, which lasted until the 1820s, taking place on Quarry Hill. An iron bullring was permanently fixed to the ground in Harewood.

Cock fighting was also extremely popular during the eighteenth century and there were numerous cockpits in town, one of which was at the *Rose and Crown Coaching Inn*. In its early days cockfights at the inn were frequent. The following advertisement appeared in the *Leeds Intelligencer* on 17 May 1757:

> *To be fought at the Rose and Crown, at the back of the Shambles, a main of cocks, betwixt the gentlemen of Leeds and the gentlemen of the West Riding. For 4 guineas the battle and 40 the main battle. To show 31 other main and 12 bye-battles. To weigh on Saturday 28th May. To fight 30th, 31st and 1st June. Feeders Abraham Farrar for Leeds and William Beeston for the West Riding.*

Even those pre-industrial leisure affairs not involving animals were usually rough in nature such as the markets and fairs of the time. Indeed, the fairs were a highlight for many of the populace, giving them a rare focal point for their leisure time. It was seen as a time to make merry and enjoy oneself.

Until the 1840s, when the Council leased land on Woodhouse Moor, just outside the town, the annual Leeds fair was held on Briggate and the land where the Holy Trinity Church would be built on Boar Lane. Zoos were still in their infancy at this time and people's curiosity about wildlife was partly satisfied through these attractions. In 1850 the fair contained about 500 animals and birds including elephants, pumas and snakes.

Throughout the eighteenth and nineteenth centuries, circuses, travelling zoos and curiosity shows were increasingly popular with lions, tigers, elephants and other large wild animals regularly on show. This could sometimes be a risky business and in November 1823 a black bear escaped from Wombwell's menagerie and made its way into the *Union Inn* on Briggate where it wreaked havoc in the bar and kitchen. Staff and customers barricaded themselves into one of the back rooms until the bear was recaptured.

A zoological park did open in Leeds in 1840 between Burley and Headingley. The zoo had plans to have all kinds of plants and many specimens of wild animals and birds, but the zoological side did not progress much further, though the grounds were well stocked with shrubs and trees. The zoo had a lake and a bear pit, but the management soon found that botany and zoology were not sufficiently popular attractions so they consulted local taste and as a result introduced more exciting attractions. This led to Madame Rossini, a tightrope walker, crossing the lake at a high altitude in a bid to bring in more punters. To further appeal to the populace, in the middle of her journey, lighted fireworks covered her in a shower of colour. Having failed in its plan to persuade the Leeds public of the merits of zoology, the zoo closed down eight years later to be replaced by a pleasure ground.

The Zoological Gardens was also the home of a Leeds gala, which was held annually whilst the park was open. It was hugely popular and in August 1842 over 12,000 people passed through its gates. The main attractions were fireworks, quite rare at this time, the centrifugal

The Bearpit on Cardigan Road in Headingley is all that remains of the Leeds Zoological Gardens of the mid-1800s. The author

railway and the laughing gas! Madame Rossini was still an attraction with her walk along the tightrope, which impressed Prince George of Cambridge who was a special guest at the gala.

In the late 1800s fairs and feasts were held in most parts of Leeds with the ones at Holbeck, Hunslet and Woodhouse Moor amongst the most popular. People flocked to have a go on the swingboats, roundabouts and flying boxes whilst others queued at the boxing rings, shooting tents and weird side-shows such as the bearded lady and the giant rat. Stalls sold food such as brandy snap, fruit nuts, hot peas, gobstoppers, toffee apples and parkin pigs.

The Leeds summer pleasure fair was another date in the diary for the Victorian public and this was a regular event at the Engineers Drill Ground on Camp Road. The most popular attractions here were the living skeleton, the fire-eaters, the tattooed lady and the man who ate glass. The fair was also famous for the talking fish and the two-tailed monkey as well as the hairless horse.

Children especially were entranced by the magic and colour which these events brought into their lives. Sydney Pickering, in his autobiography mentioned:

It was good to have a few pennies in my pocket but they were soon spent, the real attraction was to be part of the crowd under the paraffin flares and amongst the mawkers and hucksters selling their pots and pans and gaudy mechanical organs with their twitching decorated figures, striking cymbals and drums and the extravagantly carved horses and cockerels rising and falling as they went round and the great steam boat swings lifting their desperately hanging on passengers.

Drink

During the late 1700s the growing number of inns and beer houses in Leeds were the main recreational pleasure of the lower classes leading to a pastime much frowned upon by many of those who considered themselves more temperate.

The early ritualised leisure activities of cock fighting and bear baiting continued after the influx of people into newly industrialised Leeds but the new working hours produced a new formation of leisure activity, with noisy drunken riot alternating with sullen silent work.

Pubs soon began opening all over Leeds to cater for the increased demand for alcohol and the *Bingley Arms* in nearby Bardsey is credited with being one of the oldest pubs in the country. Samson Ellis was the first recorded innkeeper in 953 AD and his family remained in control until the late eighteenth century.

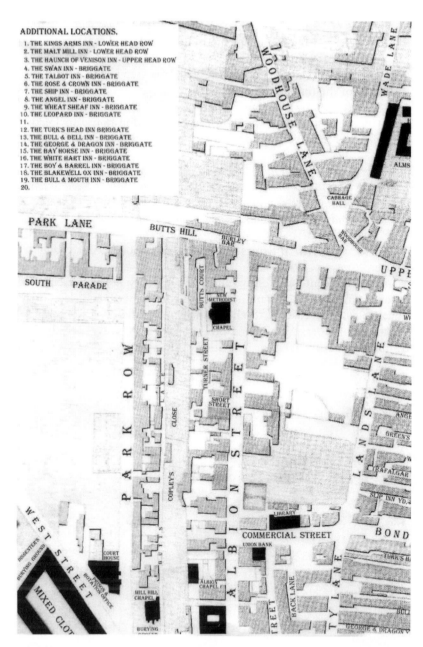

ADDITIONAL LOCATIONS.

1. THE KINGS ARMS INN - LOWER HEAD ROW
2. THE MALT MILL INN - LOWER HEAD ROW
3. THE HAUNCH OF VENISON INN - UPPER HEAD ROW
4. THE SWAN INN - BRIGGATE
5. THE TALBOT INN - BRIGGATE
6. THE ROSE & CROWN INN - BRIGGATE
7. THE SHIP INN - BRIGGATE
8. THE ANGEL INN - BRIGGATE
9. THE WHEAT SHEAF INN - BRIGGATE
10. THE LEOPARD INN - BRIGGATE
11.
12. THE TURK'S HEAD INN BRIGGATE
13. THE BULL & BELL INN - BRIGGATE
14. THE GEORGE & DRAGON INN - BRIGGATE
15. THE BAY HORSE INN - BRIGGATE
16. THE WHITE HART INN - BRIGGATE
17. THE BOY & BARREL INN - BRIGGATE
18. THE BLAKEWELL OX INN - BRIGGATE
19. THE BULL & MOUTH INN - BRIGGATE
20.

Harrison's map of Leeds showing the inns of the Upper Head Row and Briggate.
Author's collection.

The *Pack Horse* in the Pack Horse Yard off Briggate started trading in 1615 before being rebuilt in the middle of the sixteenth century. During the eighteenth century it became known as the *Slipin*, a nickname often used for popular pubs in maps of Leeds during the early part of the nineteenth century.

Ye Olde King's Arms in Lowerhead-row, as well as being one of the oldest hostelries in town was also the first posting house in Leeds. The *Yorkshire Evening Post* commented, in an article looking back:

> *Where it now stands it has stood, not always so cramped and confined by unlovely neighbours since the days when Leeds was a little town of some three or perhaps five thousand inhabitants, separated from London by a toilsome and often dangerous journey of many days.*

The *Rose and Crown* in Briggate was another famous Leeds coaching centre.

In the eighteenth and early nineteenth century it was the custom amongst the wealthy landowners to brew beer at their own households. The custom reached down to middle-class households too and innkeepers usually brewed their own ales with relatively few owning licensed properties.

Tetley's Brewery Gates. The author

The private brewing created a large demand for malt and the firm of Joshua Tetley continued to sell the product until about 1861 or 1862 by which time its brewing operation had grown to such a degree that the sale of raw materials could not be continued without reducing the stock needed for its own brewery.

By 1892 the practice of bottling beers and stouts had been established and several brewers outside of Leeds had created bottling stores within the city as they found the West Riding population enthusiastic for having their beer in this form.

As the passion for drink developed the pub became the closest thing to home for many a working man, especially for single men. For such people, their 'local' provided them with the warmth, light and shelter many of them lacked in their social lives. It also provided them with some much needed sociability, thus ensuring that the pub soon became a haven for the overcrowded urban poor.

The importance of the pub garden should not be overlooked as land and green open spaces were at a premium in the inner city and most were unable to travel to the wide open spaces of the countryside, so for many the pub garden was their one and only access to greenery.

The local pub had quickly become the social centre of its immediate neighbourhood and in the small, rural communities which made up most of Yorkshire at this time, publicans promoted games

Kirkstall Brewery. The author

Adelphi Hotel, *one of the oldest hostelries in Leeds.* The author

like skittles and 'knur and spell', as well as outdoor sports such as cricket, wrestling and football.

However, not all experiences were positive. Excessive drinking became a problem in Leeds on Saturday nights with 'labouring men staggering about or lying helpless in the gutter'. Following the Beer Act of 1830, which enabled beer to be sold even from residential premises, there was a rapid increase in the availability of drink and Leeds had over 450 beer shops by 1835.

James Hole wrote about the influence of drink within the community, saying:

Some distinction should be made between some public houses and a few more respectable beer houses, are generally well conducted, and the dram shops and lower class beerhouses. Apart from the besotting influence of the drink, the low beer house is too often the focus of depravity of a whole neighbourhood, a place where gambling and card playing constitute quite as great attractions as drinking and where prostitutes are regularly kept.

There was hostility to drink and its by-products within the Leeds Temperance movement. Temperance coffee houses, subscription concerts and circulating libraries all offered activities suitable for people away from the pub and the crowds. Religious groups including the Methodists and the Baptists also came to play an important part in the social and cultural lives of thousands of people. Church and chapel provided choirs, concerts, bands and excursions as well as the educational influence with Sunday school and bible classes.

Members of the British Women's Temperance Association were responsible for persuading men to promise never again to drink alcohol and the Band of Hope, a temperance organisation for working class children that had been founded in Leeds in 1847, also helped to increase the number of teetotallers.

Quakers and members of the Salvation Army attempted to persuade the House of Commons to pass legislation to restrict the sale of alcohol and in some parts of Britain public houses were forced to close on Sundays and permission to allow new pubs to open was restricted.

However, despite the protests of the temperance movement the number of beer-houses in Leeds almost doubled between 1826 and 1836.

There were other problems relating to the increased availability of alcohol. As Robert Baker, the noted surgeon, said in 1839:

The offensive practice which prevails, of allowing the conveniences outside public houses to remain exposed to view cannot have escaped the most casual observer.

Prostitution and gambling were also considered to be problems, accentuated by the drinking culture which had affected many within Leeds. Prostitutes were notorious in the north west of the town and it was estimated that there were thirty-seven brothels in that area alone. Gambling was another great interest and had become prevalent in the blood sports of cock fighting and bear baiting. With the introduction of horse racing as a national pastime, gambling became a greater threat and many who had won money were seen drinking away their profits in the pub whilst those who lost retreated back to their homes in a foul temper with wives and children often suffering physical harm as a result. Other forms of gambling soon followed and Leeds welcomed its first casino in Lands Lane in 1849. It was called the Leeds Casino and Concert Hall and as well as being the first casino, it was also one of the first music halls to be opened in the country.

Working men's clubs were also established in the mid-1800s. These establishments had reading rooms with newspapers and magazines where the working man could relax. Other rooms had chess or draught boards and there was also a dining area. The members of these clubs could take part in discussion classes and weekly lectures whilst there were also outdoor games and musical entertainment available.

Although drink and the pub remained a major element of working-class leisure time throughout the Victorian period, many others were not restricted solely to alcohol. Many people also enjoyed bowling, quoiting, glee clubs 'free and easies', which were the beginnings of the music hall, and amateur and professional dramatics. Others were beginning to organise fruit and vegetable shows, flower shows, sweepstake clubs, and meetings of trades and friendly societies.

Many of the pubs in the centre of Leeds during Victorian times had singing rooms and the Leeds Rational Recreation Society, founded in 1852, was instigated by middle class figures in the city in a bid to introduce 'rational recreation' to the working classes. The society sponsored many concerts at the music hall in Albion Street with a mixture of opera, ballads and comic songs.

The inns in the town did occasionally manage to pacify the temperance movement as they sometimes hired out rooms to people who wanted to show off small exhibits such as clockwork figures. Infrequent concerts and balls were the only entertainment in Leeds specifically for the gentry and a number of dancing teachers were also established in the town to teach the intricacies of country dancing.

During the 1860s there was an open street, leading from George Street, alongside the *London Tavern* into Kirkgate. On the left-hand-side was the pig market consisting of open pens and a few covered ones towards the Kirkgate end. The latter had an open roof with iron bars crossing laterally from the outside eaves to the wall and these bars afforded a good opportunity for the 'youthful gamins' who lived in the neighbourhood to practice their gymnastic exercises.

It was unbeknown to the many people who passed the area and saw the boys swinging from the bars, but these were the early days of the music halls and many of the young boys who trained on those bars found their way into the halls as gymnasts.

By the mid-1860s Leeds had at least three music halls. The casino, which had changed its name to the Amphitheatre and was now primarily a music hall, was packing in the customers. The Princes Palace opened in 1864 and the White Swan Varieties, still in existence as the City Varieties, were also in existence offering variety to the Leeds public. To cater for further cultural pursuits the Assembly Rooms were built next to the White Cloth Hall whilst the Theatre Royal opened on Hunslet Lane.

The *White Swan* coaching inn was originally built in 1750 and was bought in the 1850s by Charles Thornton who extended the singing room and created 'Thornton's New Music Hall and Fashionable

The Theatre Royal, Hunslet Lane. The author

City Varieties. The author

Lounge', opening in 1865. It changed its name thirty years later to the City Varieties.

The theatre in Hunslet Lane, which became the Theatre Royal was erected in 1771. Plays were given here by subscription, but many people in the town appeared to resent the theatre and its performers, believing to be a bad influence on the people. In one incident a young actress was crossing Leeds Bridge on her way to the theatre when she was set upon by a group of men who covered her and her gown with brown paper which they had soaked in the river. A newspaper commentating on the incident wrote, 'It appeared that any treatment was good enough for play-actor folk.'

Despite the initial hostility to the arts, the Theatre Royal, which was managed by John Coleman, managed to survive and eventually prosper in Leeds for many years until fire reduced it to ruin. The second theatre, the Amphitheatre in King Charles's Croft was also burnt down, ten months afterwards, leaving Leeds temporarily without a theatre.

The Royal Amphitheatre in Leeds was rebuilt and reopened on Saturday September 1, 1866 with a new manager Mr Henry Loraine. A cast performed the play *Macbeth* before a packed house and the *Yorkshire Post* reported:

> *We trust that Mr Loraine will meet with all encouragement he so eminently deserves. His expensive but successful effort to give the people of Leeds the opportunity of seeing Macbeth as it was no doubt intended to be seen by its great author.*

Later in 1866 the traditional pantomime reappeared at the theatre. It was called *Sinbad the sailor, of the giant ogre, the red dwarfs and the old man of the sea* and played to packed audiences during its run.

The second Theatre Royal opened its doors to the Leeds public on 2 September 1876 and a number of the top acts of the day came to Leeds for the event. It was felt significant that Leeds now had two theatres capable of attracting top acts to the area. The *Leeds Mercury* saw the opening as an indication of more prosperous times ahead:

> *We should be glad to learn that the public have supported the best work that they have been able to discriminate between real dramatic gems and past imitations but we fear that in some cases the reverse has been true. However, we are very hopeful for the future. Leeds is a great centre and is rapidly improving in matters of taste and cultivation. There can be no doubt that such a population ought to be quite able to support two well-conducted theatres.*

The Theatre Royal quickly established itself and became known for variety as well as serious drama. In 1902 it became part of the Frank MacNaghten chain of music halls before it was sold to Francis

Laidler, the pantomime king of Bradford. It was at the Theatre Royal that Charlie Chaplin and the Lancashire Lads made their name in Yorkshire at the end of the nineteenth century.

By the beginning of the 1900s there were other theatres in Leeds including the Empire Theatre in Briggate. It was here that the legendary illusionist Harry Houdini was due to appear on 6 February 1911 and he challenged local businesses to do something nobody had ever achieved: secure him so he had little chance of escape. Joshua Tetley picked up the gauntlet and challenged him to escape from a beer cask filled with bitter ale.

Houdini attempted the challenge and though he was successful, it almost ended in tragedy. A teetotaller, Houdini was overcome by the alcohol fumes and would have drowned had it not been for the help of his assistants who noticed something was wrong and pulled him out of the cask. He was only partially conscious when hauled from the container.

When the Prince Consort visited Leeds with Queen Victoria in September 1858 for the opening of the Town Hall, the town was temporarily without a theatre. He spoke to some of those present about the progress of Leeds and the culture of the 'capital of the West Riding' and asked, 'have you a good theatre?' to which the answer was no. The Prince is reported to have replied: 'You should have one for nothing is more calculated to promote the culture and raise the tone of the people.'

Sir Peter Fairburn, who was among those listening to the Prince, responded to the challenge and though plans were already in place for the rebuilding of the Royal Amphitheatre and the Theatre Royal, he was anxious to promote a scheme for the erection of a 'temple of drama' for the West Riding. Other people soon became involved in the project and a large, convenient site in New Briggate, which amounted to three-quarters of an acre was secured with plans drawn up. Work on the new building began in early October 1877 at a cost of over £60,000.

The Leeds papers were unanimous in their belief that the plans for the Grand Theatre were on a more complete and elaborate scale than any other city in the kingdom. The *Yorkshire Post* said:

> *Drury Lane, Covent Garden and Her Majesties have not got the stage room of the Grand, nor are they so beautifully shaped or so comfortable for the audiences. The building seems perfectly unique, not only among English playhouses, but amongst those of other countries.*

The Grand Theatre. The author

On Saturday, 16 November 1878, a limited number of people, by invitation only were able to get a preview of the wonder of the Grand Theatre and on Monday 18 November the theatre was finally opened to the public with a production of *Much Ado About Nothing*. Every seat had been sold weeks before and many people were disappointed. When the curtains finally rose, Mr Barratt, the manager of the theatre addressed those present from the stage. He said:

> *Ladies and gentleman. I heartily welcome you to this, one of the finest if not the finest theatre in Europe. That cheer of yours rather makes me feel like the naughty boy who got a prize by mistake. This magnificent theatre was built, not by me but by the enterprise of your townsmen and by the architects Messrs Corson and Watson.*

The levels of comfort were variable throughout the theatre as only the best seats could be booked whilst the rest had to queue. The back stalls were then known as the pit, with long wooden seats and a wooden plank for a backrest. Admission to the pit was one shilling, but for an extra sixpence people were allowed to sit by the 'early doors'. If the pit filled up a man came round and forced his way between people in a bid to make more room.

The Grand mainly presented pre and post-London West End productions whilst the Theatre Royal, when it re-opened, was the home of the melodrama and popular pantomime.

People's leisure time was altered by the onset of the industrial revolution with free weekends, added to with the occasional Monday holidays for saint's days. Football was increasingly popular and was played at three o'clock on a Saturday afternoon. This was because providers of space were nearly always employers or the church, so workers had to put in a shift on Saturday mornings, and Sundays were for religious activities, leaving Saturday afternoon as the only free time.

Sundays became the only common free day for working men to spend with their families, though many women did not have the luxury of a rest on this day with most being forced to spend their time on domestic activities such as washing. For those who were able to venture out of the house, brass bands, which became a feature of religious parades, electioneering and sporting occasions, were also regularly seen in public parks on a Sunday afternoon. Roundhay Park, although condemned as a waste of money when the town purchased part of the Nicholson Estate in 1871, eventually became regarded as a real asset, helped greatly by the tram route which soon linked it to the rest of Leeds.

By the middle of the 1800s there was more free time for workers due to new factory legislation and at the same time railways were making more of the country accessible including the coastal towns.

BOATHOUSE AND LAKE, ROUNDHAY PARK, LEEDS.

Roundhay Park opened in 1871 but became truly popular after a tram route linked it to other parts of Leeds. Author's collection

This led to fishing ports such as Scarborough, Bridlington, Whitby and Filey becoming increasingly attractive to the workers of Leeds and establishing themselves as popular seaside resorts.

The beaches filled up during the summer months with row upon row of deck chairs lining the promenade. Children were kept amused by the Punch and Judy shows whilst the adults were entertained by the pierrots and negro minstrels.

Christmas-time in Leeds was observed by appropriate services in the churches and chapels and in many of them advantage was taken of the occasion to make collections on behalf of the sufferers of recent wars or natural disasters. The inmates of the workhouse were annually treated to a large Christmas dinner while the scholars of the

Mansion House, Roundhay Park. Built by Thomas Nicholson in 1818. The author

Leeds Ragged and Industrial Schools and the patients of the general infirmary were also able to participate in Christmas.

Most houses were decorated with streamers, paper flowers and balls which the children helped to make and which were displayed alongside holly and mistletoe. Many had Christmas trees decorated with small, wax candles. The children went carol singing, collecting pennies and in the Christmas stocking for many were a new penny, an apple and an orange, some sweets and perhaps a small toy such as a clockwork train.

After a large Christmas dinner and a high tea with pies, hams and cakes, people played games including blindman's buff, animal, vegetable or mineral, postman's knock or charades.

The Leeds City Art Gallery was the inspiration of Colonel Walter Harding who bought and presented paintings at the gallery as well as persuading other notable citizens to donate their works of art. The gallery was opened as a £9,000 addition to George Corson's Municipal Buildings on 31 October 1888 by the Lord Mayor, Archibald Scarr.

John Atkinson Grimshaw became a popular artist in Leeds, largely known for his still life's with a few landscapes of the Leeds area. These paintings often included the smoke pollution and damp fogs that were common in industrial cities in the late nineteenth century. Grimshaw had campaigned for a Leeds City Art Gallery since it was first suggested in the mid-1850s and the gallery mounted annual spring exhibitions in which Grimshaw was always represented.

The cafés of Leeds became amongst the city's most popular attractions in the early part of the twentieth century. People used to go there for lunch whilst others gathered merely to socialise in a new setting, drinking tea, though the drinking of coffee increased in popularity as the café culture grew. The people of Leeds also attended the cafés to listen to the music on offer. At one of the cafés was an orchestra of eight musicians including a pianist, two violinists and a cello player.

One of the most enduring cultural contributions to the city is the Leeds Library which opened in 1768. It eventually moved to its present home in Commercial Street and is today the oldest surviving example of a subscription library left in England.

10   Law and Order

Even in medieval times, the fledgling settlement of Leeds needed law and order to ensure that some semblance of society was maintained. Thefts, land disputes and murders were crimes which needed punishment from the Middle Ages, yet there was no effective body to fight crime. Manorial courts were able to deal with relatively minor matters but serious crimes had to be dealt with by another body usually the county sheriff, the Justices of the Peace or the higher courts of the country. At this time, with Leeds still a largely agricultural area, fights and other forms of lawlessness were rife.

It was the Justices of the Peace who carried most authority before the police force came into effect. However, their work was not limited to administering criminal law. They also ruled on poor relief, set wages and ensured that vagabonds were flogged, therefore the need for a force solely responsible for upholding the law was necessary long before the Leeds Police Force was formed.

One of the first vices to take a grip on the people of Leeds was gambling, it was especially a problem in the eighteenth century and the papers of the time urged action to be taken on habits which saw the winners spending their gains in the local ale-houses whilst the loser 'vents his ill humours on his wife and poor children.'

It was a violent age though people were made aware of the consequences of illegal activity. In March 1736 the *Leeds Mercury* noted that the theft of some hops from a property in Nosthorpe carried the death penalty.

Street brawls were prevalent and at times there appeared to be little to prevent grievances amongst a section of the population degenerating into mob violence. This was amply demonstrated in 1735 when the rise in the price of corn led to riots across the country including Leeds with several people killed in the disturbances.

In 1755 an act was passed for lighting the streets and regulating the pavements of Leeds. The act acknowledged that several burglaries, robberies and other disorders had occurred in the town and that such an act would be of great benefit in helping to prevent further law breaking.

As the eighteenth century continued industrialisation began to spread in Britain. The country was slowly metamorphosising from being largely agricultural into one increasingly dominated by urban conurbations and industry. Great wealth came to many, though that also had an adverse effect in the gap between rich and poor which widened considerably.

Thus the issue of poverty became a serious one in Leeds. In 1820, out of a population of between 30,000 and 40,000, it was estimated that at least 7,000 lived in 'abject penury and wretchedness'. This in turn had an effect on the crime rate which duly rose with the number of people seeking new measures to try and relieve themselves of their parlous situation. Children were sent out to steal whatever they could find and the problem of theft became so bad that a night watch was appointed in town.

Prostitution was another by-product of the terrible poverty. One of the worst examples of this time was in May 1804 when a man sold his wife for five guineas to another 'acquainted with her merits'. In some of the poorer areas of Leeds, there were many 'houses of vice', the forerunner of brothels. It became another issue to trigger a divide between the poorer members of the town and those who came to be regarded as 'respectable'.

Leeds Prison was originally situated at the north end of Middle Row and was then called Capon Hall. In 1655 the prison was removed to a building in the middle of Kirkgate, just by the entrance into Briggate. The building was a two-storey affair with five or six cells and the jailor lived in the house adjoining the prison. It was a

Cartoon showing a prisoner in a Leeds cell. West Yorkshire Archive Service

decrepit building even by the standards of the time, being without a sewer, fireplace or even glazed windows.

Towards the end of the eighteenth century, John Fish managed to juggle the role of being the Chief Constable along with also being the keeper of the keys of the prison and the keeper of the town's fire engine, which was stored in the prison.

At this time, most prisons were not places to incarcerate people who had committed grievous crimes, as the fate of murderers was to hang apart from unique mitigating circumstances. Small offences were settled by a period in the stocks, worse ones by the pillory and cases of petty theft by whippings from a cart tail and a branding with a red hot iron on the hand. The more serious cases including stealing, highway robbery, forgery and murder were taken to York where the defendants fate, if found guilty, would be death by hanging.

In 1811 the Leeds Corporation was being urged to take action on the state of the prison and places where the affairs of the town were conducted including the police court. The town's meetings were held at the Moot Hall which was in the middle of Briggate. Police courts were set up here twice a week to deal with the minor misdemeanors

Moot Hall, where the courts were originally situated. From an ingraving by Charles Heath, 1816. Brian Elliott collection

which affected Leeds. Both the prison and the Moot Hall were felt inadequate for the growing town, so in 1811 a proper court house was built with a prison attached. The building, opposite Mill Hill Chapel with the entrance in Park Row, was opened in 1813.

At the courthouse the main business of the town was conducted until the opening of the Town Hall in 1858. It also held the Quarterly Sessions and the daily magistrates court.

The courts of the time were busy and crime was an issue which grew in prominence as the early years of the nineteenth century passed. More letters appeared in the local papers on the subject and more meetings took place to try and address the issue. By this time Leeds had become home to a barracks, a factor which appeared to lead to an escalation of the problem.

Some people in the town were concerned, even at this relatively early stage, at the undeniable link between social deprivation and crime. One such person was Richard Oastler who himself was born and bred in the slum area of Quarry Hill. He wrote a number of letters to the *Leeds Mercury* during 1830 describing the terrible conditions in which children as young as seven were having to work. His prompting led directly to Shaftesbury's Factories Act of 1833

Marsh Lane Police Station. Leeds City Libraries

which made it illegal for factories to employ children under the age of nine, and reduced to forty-eight the number of hours that children under the age of thirteen were able to work.

Throughout the eighteenth century there were unpaid constables who were there to try and stem the growing tide of lawlessness but it was apparent that further action needed to be taken. Laws on Woodhouse Moor were solely upheld by the constable on duty there and the bellringer, however the constable was not bound to attend to any disturbance when called for unless the messenger produced a shilling. With the Luddites wreaking havoc in the country and people increasingly desperate both at work and at home, the Leeds police force was founded in 1836 under the leadership of Chief Constable Edward Read.

Though primarily concerned with the fighting of crime, the force largely became known, at least in the early days, as one to be paraded on ceremonial occasions and the officers were also trained as fire-fighters.

The force was in for a tough baptism as the increasing population, recurring economic crises, widespread poverty, appalling working

The original sketch of the Woodhouse Police Station. Leeds City Libraries

and living conditions and political agitation posed problems the town had difficulty in coping with. Luddite riots broke out in Leeds in 1812 and again in 1842 when military intervention was required to support the newly formed force in suppressing a Chartist insurrection. Meanwhile, mass demonstrations on Holbeck Moor were a response to the government's refusal to introduce some aspect of Parliamentary Reform.

The Chartist movement was formed as a reaction to the poor social and economic conditions of the mid-1800s and it was to provide the newly formed Leeds police with an early test.

Every elector in the borough was called upon to act as a special constable, so a force of between six and eight thousand was hoped for. Nearly all the mill-hands were sworn in early.

Riots over working conditions broke out in Hunslet, Holbeck and the west of Leeds and a police contingent was sent from the courthouse to attempt to intercept the mob, led by Edward Read on horseback. A force of special constables, numbering about 1,200 was in the contingent along with members of the Royal Horse Artillery. In Holbeck and again in Dewsbury Road, the mob and the police clashed, with the Chief Constable attacked and missiles thrown at the police. Eventually, with the arrival of the special constables, the force was able to overpower the opposition and several of the men were taken into custody.

The main streets were thronging with people and large number of special constables patrolled the streets by day whilst the infantry took over by night. A big new building in front of the *White Horse Inn* in Boar Lane was used as a temporary barracks and rooms were used in every ward of Leeds for the accommodation of the army of special constables.

The force was kept busy even when the threat from the Chartist movement had subsided. In an incident in June 1844 when two soldiers from the 70th Regiment of Foot were arrested after attacking a man, disturbances were triggered off after several of their colleagues at the barracks had tried to rescue them. Heavy fighting ensued around the town centre and, though their rescuers freed the two men for a time, they were soon re-arrested in Briggate.

However this did not quell the disturbances as between forty and fifty of their fellow soldiers escaped from their barracks in Woodhouse Street and gathered at the *Green Parrot* public house in Harper Street. When evening broke they marched further into town armed with sticks and bludgeons looking for an encounter with the police. Fighting ensued in the centre of town and many of the special forces were injured, though order was eventually restored through a military presence.

One of the most infamous incidents involving the police became known as the Dripping Riot. A cook in Leeds stole some dripping from his employers' and was given what appeared to be a very heavy sentence of a month in prison, a decision which led to a crowd gathering around the house in which he was arrested. Five men were arrested after the incident.

In 1842 the Great Potato Famine hit Ireland, an event which devastated the economy leading to widespread poverty amongst the populace. In desperation, many families began to move away from the country with large numbers making the short journey across the Irish Sea to England.

By 1861 many had found their way to Leeds with twelve and a half per cent of the population of Leeds then being of Irish origin. Most of those who came over settled in the Bank area to the east of the town.

The immigration led to a crimewave in this part of town and Irish immigrants were estimated to be responsible for at least fourteen per cent of the cases which came before the Leeds Quarter Sessions between 1851 and 1861. The influx of Irish people caused tension in the local community, adding to what was already widespread mistrust of the Catholic Church and the atmosphere between Leeds residents and the new immigrants took a turn for the worse.

The Fenians was the short title for the Irish Republican Brotherhood, a nationalist movement founded in New York in 1857. A forerunner to Sinn Fein/IRA, the movement advocated violence as a means of achieving its objectives and it was illegal to be a member of the group in the UK.

The Fenians were infamous for their attacks in London and Manchester which became known as the 'Fenian Outrages'. In September 1865 James McCarthy, a workman at Lawsons engineers in Mabgate, was brought before the mayor, on the suspicion that he was the Secretary of the Leeds Fenian Society. He was cautioned but mistrust between the two communities continued and was soon to reach boiling point.

Early in 1866 large numbers of Irishmen left Leeds, Bradford, Halifax and Huddersfield apparently with the intention of meeting with fellow Fenians in Chester, their alleged aim being to raid the large store of arms in the castle and start an uprising. The Home Secretary rushed Police and troops to Chester and some 1,200 men of 'very doubtful character' were dispersed.

That same night a police constable at Wellington Street railway Station saw a young man carrying a bulky parcel of 'suspicious appearance'. He followed the man into Basinghall Street and challenged him. The parcel consisted of twenty-four packages containing 140 ball cartridges, all greased and ready for use. Two days later, on 13 February, packages of rifle cartridges were found in the Morley railway tunnel – probably having been thrown from a train on the way back from Chester.

There appeared little doubt that the Nationalist group posed a great threat to the safety of officers as well as the population at large and disturbances continued throughout 1866 and into 1867 culminating in the murder of Police Sergeant Brett in Manchester. Those responsible for the murder were arrested, charged and found guilty. It was their subsequent execution which in turn caused outrage amongst the Irish community in England including Leeds.

On 13 December 1867 large placards with black borders were posted all over Leeds and marches in support of the Fenian movement were organised to take place in the centre of town, in support of those who had been charged with the murder of the police officer.

It had been intended for demonstrators to hold up placards with the legend:

God save Ireland! Irishmen of Leeds, you are called upon to do a sacred duty, follow the noble example of your countrymen throughout the country and Ireland. Attend in thousands in the Vicar's Croft on Sunday next. Your manhood and patriotism depend on your meeting. Irish women, show your husbands a noble example by your attendance in thousands. All who can attend are expected. Let your actions tend to the maintenance of order and prove that you appreciate the object of your meeting. Let your rallying cry be Allen, Larkin and O'Brien.

The Leeds Volunteers were called upon to be ready should any violence occur and large crowds gathered in Leeds to watch the events with the mounted special constables present in large numbers. As 150 infantrymen of the 70th Regiment waited at the Corn Exchange, a battery of Royal Artillery were drawn up in front of the White Cloth Hall, guarded by a detachment of infantry with rifles. The Leeds Squadron of yeomanry was nearby, led by the Earl of Harewood.

The police took possession of Vicar's Croft and drew up in double line at the entrances to Kirkgate, George Street and Ludgate Hill while magistrates stood nearby at Vicar's Croft and the Corn Exchange. The mayor, Darnton Lupton, presided over this army on horseback and all was silent as the Town Hall clock struck twice. However, no procession started.

The streets in and around Kirkgate, had by the Sunday resumed their usual appearance, though there were perhaps one or two more people walking around. All the extra policemen had been withdrawn, though large bodies of constables were massed at the Town Hall and at the divisional stations. There was widespread relief that the mass demonstration did not take place and credit was given to the Catholic clergy for the fact that the anger had not spilt over into great conflict.

By the nineteenth century Leeds began to be in need of a new prison and at a cost of £43,000 a plot of land in Armley was purchased. Armley Gaol opened in July 1847 and, perched on a hill, the prison could clearly be seen in the centre of town and presented an imposing sight. By this time the population of Leeds had risen to well over 100,000 and the prison was desperately needed to reduce the pressure on the police cells.

When the Town Hall was completed in 1858 the courts and administration of the police were transferred from the old Court House and by May 1864 all the West Riding Assizes were held in Leeds.

HMP Leeds 'The Early Years'. West Yorkshire Archive Service

Armley Gaol, built in 1847. West Yorkshire Archive Service

The new Chief Constable of Leeds, James Wetherell was able to give precise figures on offenders in Leeds in 1867 which gives a good indication on the main crimes affecting Leeds at that time. He said in a statement that there were 479 known thieves, 38 receivers of stolen goods, 293 prostitutes and 590 suspicious characters together with a continuous stream of vagrants and tramps, numbering over 970 on the streets of Leeds on one night alone.

The Chief Constable said that with the increasing population of the town, the settlement of previously convicted thieves in the biggest, most populous neighbourhoods, the task of diminishing crime has been made even more difficult.

He condemned the drinking culture which he said was prevalent in Leeds at the time and said it was to be regretted that:

people comparatively destitute of moral training should have such facilities afforded for them. For spirit drinking, that is now the case by the

The Victoria Hotel, *built in 1865 to serve people attending the Assizes Courts which were then held at Leeds Town Hall.* The author

> *ever increasing though much to be condemned custom of indiscriminately introducing dram shops into public houses. Robbed of almost every proper feeling by reckless dram drinking, a practice too much encouraged in the lowest of these places, ignorant and dissipated persons frequently commit crime without a motive. Save a savage impulse excited by excessive indulgence in intoxicated liquors.*

Strikes struck Leeds during 1913 and one involving council workers in December especially affected police. It led to violence when non-union labour was drafted in to try and keep services running. Demonstrators had to be kept apart from the new labour and the

Cartoon showing prisoners arriving at Leeds prison. West Yorkshire Archive Service

situation deteriorated further when bombs were planted at a Crown Point power station and at Harewood Barracks. Demands on the time of the average police officer meant that all were employed on twelve-hour shifts every day.

The suffragette movement caused further pressure on the force, notably when Herbert Asquith arrived in the city as Prime Minister. Women were not allowed into the meeting he was addressing at the Coliseum, but some protestors at the railway station intercepted him. He was then followed by a number of activists, especially Jenny Baines who challenged him. She was arrested, along with four others and charged with unlawful assembly and inciting riot and sedition.

As the force went into the twentieth century the then Chief Constable of Leeds, Major Tarry, perhaps noting the tensions which had existed between the force and the Irish immigrants, reacted to the large Jewish immigration into Leeds in the early 1900s by suggesting that some of his force should learn to speak Yiddish. It was an idea that had originated from London where the largest Jewish community in the country lived. Police work with the community in Leeds had to go through an interpreter as the vast majority of those coming into the country did not speak English.

This century has seen the work with ethnic communities increasing and the task of the police, in maintaining law and order, as challenging as it was when the force was first seen on the streets of Leeds.

11 *W*ARTIME LEEDS

During the 1600s Leeds was a bastion of non-conformity and was generally favourable to the parliamentary cause. However it was nearby Bradford which was controlled by the Parliament whilst Leeds was a stronghold of forces loyal to the King.

Arguments intensified between the Royalists and the Parliamentarians and the Roundheads and Cavaliers and in August 1642 King Charles I raised his standard at Nottingham and the Civil War began with Leeds heavily involved. As soon as the conflict began, Leeds was garrisoned by the Kings troops but an attack on the town took place to the south of Leeds Bridge, near to the start of Buhr Lane (Boar Lane).

Sir William Savile held the town for the Royalists with their main camp located at Cavalier Hill but after attacking parliamentary forces in Bradford they were repulsed and retreated back to Leeds with the main battles taking place at the fortifications near St John's Church. By 1643 parliamentary forces were marching steadily towards Leeds, gathering on Woodhouse Moor where the University now stands.

Six troops of horses, three companies of dragoons, one thousand musketeers and two thousand clubmen were led by Sir Thomas Fairfax who had marched through Bradford on his way to taking control of Leeds.

With parliamentary forces advancing from Woodhouse Moor and another section coming from Hunslet their forces were in the ascendancy. Savile was asked to surrender but refused and the Royalists were finally driven out of town with about forty killed. Fairfax led his men into the heart of Leeds and 500 prisoners were taken by his Parliamentary troops. However, they were released on a promise never to serve against the parliamentarians in the future. Cannons and quantities of gunpowder were left behind by the royalists.

King Charles I. Royal.gov.uk

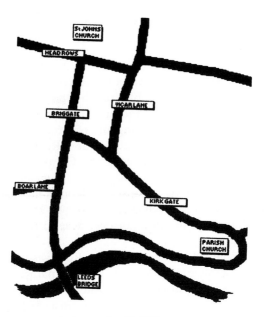

Map of the battle in Leeds during the Civil War. The author

This did not signal the end to the conflict however as the Royalists took Leeds once again in 1643 before Fairfax regained control a year later. The war badly affected the town with many properties in ruin, little food available and trade going elsewhere to those towns unaffected by war. In addition, the public health of the town was in an appalling state and disease was rife.

Leeds was to brace itself for war once again in the seventeenth century. Charles Edward Stuart, otherwise known as 'Bonnie Prince Charlie' was the grandson of the deposed Catholic King James II, who had fled from Protestant William of Orange's invading army in 1688.

There was strong support for the deposed King, especially in the Highlands and Islands of Scotland. The Stuarts were desperate to reclaim the throne and in 1745, Charles travelled to the Highlands to raise the clans in rebellion. His plan was to make his father King.

On the night of 5 November, Leeds folk were out on the streets celebrating Guy Fawkes Night when word spread that Bonnie Prince Charlie and his men had crossed the Tweed and were heading south. In a panic, the streets quickly emptied and the people of Leeds stayed behind their front doors, hiding away their valuables and praying for better news.

A Leeds Parliament was formed and a corps of a hundred troops was arranged to try and defend the city from the rebel attack. General George Wade came north, briefed to subdue the clans and prevent another rebellion. His solution was to build roads good enough to cart cannon into the heart of the Highlands which would repel any threat from north of the border.

General Wade pitched his tents between Sheepscar and Woodhouse, which was the base of his operations against the invasion. Meanwhile it was becoming clear that support from English Jacobites was not emerging as Charles had hoped. Government armies were gathering and the military situation looked increasingly bleak. Eventually the Jacobites retreated back to Scotland, and Wade Lane and Camp Road are reminders of the last time that Leeds was forced to defend itself against attack from north of the border.

Sir Thomas Fairfax, 1612–1671. Author's collection

During the American War of Independence in 1776 the *Leeds Intelligencer* reported that men from the West Riding were joining up with the intention of bringing 'the ungrateful colonists to their duty'. However, opinion in the city was divided, not least because of the likely effect on the town's burgeoning textile trade with tradesmen saying that due to the conflict, the 'distresses of the labouring Poor are very

General George Wade. Spartacus Educational

much increased'. The town continued to suffer great divisions throughout the war with some burning effigies of George Washington and Benjamin Franklin and lighting candles in windows to celebrate when the war was going well. There was anger at those who refused to celebrate and many who had refused to put candles in their windows, had to suffer the distress of seeing their windows smashed by an angry mob.

Leeds was once again prepared for conflict as the eighteenth century drew to an end. In February 1793 the French declared war on Britain and the whole country, including the West Riding, was bracing itself for the very real possibility of a French invasion. There was the added threat, to those in authority, that the lower classes would rise up and attempt to overthrow the ruling elite in imitation of the French working classes.

As a response to both threats, a group of loyal townsmen were called for and the Leeds Volunteers created. In May 1795 some 60,000 people gathered on Chapeltown Moor to witness the arrival of the Leeds Volunteers and other forces from the West Riding ready for conflict.

Banks in the city held appeals for the widows and orphans of those killed in conflict. However, as in the American War of Independence,

Map of Leeds in the eighteenth century. Author's collection

trade suffered and those in industry opposed the war and urged a peaceful end to the conflict.

It appeared that their wish had been granted in October 1801 when a situation of stalemate existed. The French may have dominated Europe but the British navy controlled the seas and the threat of an invasion from across the English Channel subsided. People tumbled out onto the streets of Leeds to celebrate the end of hostilities. Sheep were roasted whole on spits and large amounts of brown stout were drunk.

However, peace was short-lived and in May 1803 Britain declared war on France. The Leeds Volunteers attempted to reform and they were divided into two battalions of infantry and two troops of Volunteer Cavalry. Equipment and uniform came as a result of donations from the people of Leeds. In preparation for a possible invasion, a number of beacons were positioned throughout the country with the Leeds beacon being placed on Seacroft Moor Top.

The people of Leeds longed for peace and a petition was arranged with 26,628 people signing it in calling for peace. In June 1815, the news came through of the victory at Waterloo and Napoleon's surrender. Once again people poured onto the streets, more in relief than celebration as the war had taken a heavy toll on the town. The lower classes suffered more from the poor trading climate of the time due to a combination of rising unemployment and higher food prices. Also, Leeds was a tense and a nervous town after almost two decades of war. Poverty was rife, as was social disharmony.

However, the twentieth century brought no respite from conflict and Leeds, as with the rest of the country, was affected by the Second Boer War which ended in June 1902. Over 21,000 British servicemen died in the conflict with many hailing from the West Riding. When the conflict came to an end a special edition of the *Yorkshire Evening Post* was rushed onto the streets so that the rumour, which had infected the city, could be finally confirmed.

After a few precious years of peace, Britain declared war on Germany on 4 August 1914 and all over the country men were waving goodbye to their families in readiness for their departure into battle. In Leeds, men in the city were immediately urged to take the 'King's Shilling' and there was a campaign aimed at recruiting many of those ready, willing and able to assist their country. Cinemas tried to recruit after films ended and possible recruits were invited onto the pitch after a Leeds City match at Elland Road. About 1,200 volunteers enrolled in the 15th Battalion of the West Yorkshire Regiment which became known as the 'Leeds Pals'.

People celebrating after the Relief of Mafeking. Thoresby Society

The campaign worked and a month into the war more than 5,000 Leeds men had volunteered. To continue the recruiting campaign the Leeds Joint Parliamentary Recruiting Committee was set up to encourage more Leeds men to volunteer for the forces. Voluntary workers paid over 200,000 visits, obtaining promises from men to enlist. By August 1915 there were over 47,000 Leeds men who had joined up and by the end of the 1914–18 war over 82,000 men had been recruited in the city.

Those left behind were faced with living in a city on a war footing. School children dug up fields to turn them into allotments and collected eggs to be given to military hospitals. Special constables kept a nightly watch on a city plunged into darkness as the street lights had been dimmed. Food rationing was introduced in 1917 whilst pubs reduced their opening hours and watered down their beer.

With so many men away from the city at war, women took over in many industries and ensured the running of the city in the absence of the servicemen. Harewood House, meanwhile, became an auxiliary hospital for officers.

Though Leeds was not as badly hit as some cities, it was still a target for bombs and a munitions factory was hit in December 1915 killing thirty-five female workers. In the autumn of 1916 a bomb was dropped on a park at Harewood and another hit nearby Collingham.

However, 1 July 1916 was the worst day of the war for the city of Leeds even though no bombs fell on the city. The Leeds Pals regiment took part in the Battle of the Somme in an attempt to break through the German lines. There were 57,000 British casualties on that first day of conflict and of the 900 Leeds Pals who entered battle, only seventeen returned home.

Those who remained to keep the home fires burning literally did so. A record 226 million tonnes of coal was excavated from the Yorkshire Coalfield whilst production at the first National Shell Factory at Armley rose to 10,000 shells a week.

The first convoy of wounded soldiers arrived back in Leeds on 17 September 1914, having taken part in the Battle of the Marne. A crowd of 6,000 watched them being taken from City Square to Beckett's Park. The high casualty rate meant that accommodation for the wounded became very scarce and in 1915 the old workhouse in Beckett Street was converted into a 500-bed hospital.

As a major industrial city, Leeds became an important centre for the production of war materials and the textile industry adapted for the common cause. It was especially prominent in the manufacture of uniforms whilst the manufacturing industry turned out components for weapons, aeroplanes, tanks and military vehicles.

Food prices rose steadily during the war, although rationing did not take effect until the latter stages of the conflict. Between June 1914 and the June of 1917, fish rose in price by 134 per cent and bacon by eighty per cent. The war had taken its toll on home life in the city but all was forgotten on 11 November 1918 as the armistice was announced. However, amidst all the bonfires which were lit and the fireworks let off, there was an appreciation that there were many grieving widows and children amongst the masses. Of the 82,000 men who had left Leeds in 1914, there were 9,640 who were never to return home.

During 1938, as the tensions in Europe increased once again, Leeds went back onto a war footing. Into the following year, as war became inevitable, it was a sombre city which prepared, once again, to defend itself from attack. A disused water main was discovered in which 5,000 people could be accommodated in the event of an attack on the city and throughout Leeds people were busy digging trenches and erecting air raid shelters.

A recruiting drive for ARP wardens had been made in 1939 and local volunteers were trained to support the efforts of the Leeds City Police Fire Service. Air-raid shelters were also erected throughout the city and by 1939 over 14,000 had been built, capable of giving protection to 300,000 people.

In August 1939, just days before war was declared on Germany, Leeds City Art Gallery and museum staff were preoccupied with ensuring that city treasures were protected from the likely bombings.

Gas masks were issued to school children and on 1 September 1939, two days before the declaration of war, 18,250 children and 2,800 teachers and voluntary workers were evacuated from Leeds on fifty-one special trains, mainly to Lincolnshire and the Yorkshire Dales. A day later they were followed by 8,000 mothers, pregnant women and disabled people, all to nearby areas thought to be less at risk of attack than the industrial heartland of West Yorkshire.

Children preparing to leave the city swarmed around the man selling comics near the train station at Leeds City North. Amid cries of 'give us a comic mister' the travellers set off on their journey, with little noticeable sign of emotion. To many it was a big adventure and they were mostly unaware of the grave threat posed to Britain in the coming weeks, months and years.

Thousands of the children arrived at Pateley Bridge and other parts of North Yorkshire with teachers there to greet them at the station. Doctors, nurses and ambulance workers and other helpers were also gathered ready to give assistance where needed.

The children were told that they were going on holiday with the teachers who tried to enter into the spirit of the occasion, hoping to ensure that their young charges remained as stress-free as possible.

However, the relocation turned out to be unpopular as the theory grew that the risk of war was not quite as serious as that put forward by the government. After the air-raid siren on the day war was declared, there appeared little imminent threat and by the time schools reopened in January 1940, half of the evacuees had returned home.

However, the 'phoney' war lasted only until the spring of 1940 when the German army swept across Europe, eventually taking Paris.

British forces had to evacuate from Dunkirk with about 20,000 troops coming to Leeds to board with civilians.

With the Battle of Britain still to come, the threat of an invasion by the German army was strong and Leeds took precautions. Sandbag barricades were erected in front of key city buildings and many windows were protected to prevent them shattering in the event of an explosion. Any scrap of metal, from railings to pots and pans was gathered up and collected for the war effort.

War memorial to the servicemen who fought for the 'Leeds Rifles in the two world wars'. The author

The first of four million ration books had been distributed throughout the city in November 1939 and in the following year Leeds became the first city to hold a 'War Weapons Week'. It was set up to raise money for the armed forces with its target being 250 bombers. City Square hosted the event and a large 'Barometer Board' in the square gave a visual illustration of how many bombers had been bought.

The Town Hall had an air raid shelter and a British Restaurant in the cellar during the war. British Restaurants existed in cities across Britain, and were an attempt to ensure the provision of wholesome meals for the populace.

Throughout 1940 and the following year, Leeds took a pounding from the Luftwagge as thousands of incendiaries and bombs rained down on the city causing huge damage.

The first raid on Leeds by the Luftwaffe in September 1940 saw an estimated 4,000 incendiaries and fourteen high explosives fall on the city. In an industrial area of the city a fractured gas main, caused by one of the bombs, started a fire which rapidly spread into a brilliant blaze, lighting up the night sky until it was quickly subdued. A modern inn nearby was severely damaged, and older premises on the opposite side of the road were demolished with the ruins set on fire. A lock-up shop nearby was also hit and burnt out. In this raid one civilian was killed, and among other casualties was an air-raid warden who lost a leg.

A large audience at a cinema had a remarkable escape on the same night. A bomb which struck the building fell within about ten minutes of their departure. It penetrated the roof and fell directly onto the seats in the cinema. Luckily, the film had finished and the cinema was deserted with no casualties reported.

The attacks led to panic amongst the people. The 'phoney war' was at an end and a walk through the shattered streets brought home the grim reality of conflict. Those who had not previously applied for air raid shelters now did so urgently and met with a cool response from the city authority.

There was worse to come for the city with widespread enemy raids throughout the night on 14 March 1941. Papers reported that at least two enemy bombers were shot down and though not able to identify which areas had been worst affected, they reported that the North East of England had been badly affected with a town badly hit.

Shortly before midnight high explosives and incendiaries were showered over the city. The telephone system was put out of action immediately and the waterworks and gas supplies affected. There was damage to the City Museum and those who passed the smouldering museum after the raid recalled a scattering of mounted butterflies from the collections. 4,600 houses were damaged, 100 of them beyond repair and a bomb damaged the Judges Chambers in the Town Hall shortly before its clock struck midnight.

Wellington Street was a major target and it had City Station, a goods yard and timber yard affected. Also, one of the main hotels in the city received a direct hit from a high explosive bomb on the same night. Considerable damage was done to the top floor, but no one was seriously hurt. Early in the raid a high explosive hit the entrance to the emergency receiving department at a hospital. Some casualties were just being received when the bomb fell and doctors and nurses worked throughout the raid, whilst members of the hospital staff went out and rescued three men from a building in the vicinity. Casualty figures were often obscured in wartime to deny the Germans propaganda material but post-war records suggest sixty-five people were killed that night and 260 injured, fifty-six of them seriously.

At the time of the Second World War, Leeds was a major centre for textiles, clothing, optics and heavy engineering, so it had a skilled workforce who were soon needed for the war effort.

Much of the city's industrial output was used in making fuses, shells and field guns. Tanks were made at Royal Ordnance Barnbow and John Fowler's Steam Plough Works. Hunslet Engine Company remodelled a pre-war design to produce the 'Austerity' shunter, a stripped down locomotive, which was to prove instrumental in the eventual liberation of Europe.

The textile factories of Leeds were heavily reliant on a female workforce. However, as many men left the city for combat, more women began to take on jobs traditionally done by the men. So women began to turn their hands to necessities such as machining and forgework.

Waddingtons, Leeds-based manufacturers of board games such as Monopoly did its bit for the war effort by supplying games and playing cards to British POWs. These included hidden maps to aid escape.

A battered, bruised but unbowed Leeds received a welcome boost on 16 May 1942 when the wartime Prime Minister, Winston Churchill, arrived unexpectedly and spent three hours talking with local officials before finding time to deliver an unprepared speech to 20,000 from the steps of Leeds Town Hall. Later, Churchill, waving the ubiquitous cigar, and his wife were driven round the streets in an open car.

During the Second World War a total of seventy-seven people were killed by bombs in Leeds and 197 buildings were destroyed. Between 25 August 1940 and 28 August 1942 alone there were nine bombing raids on Leeds with eighty-seven alerts. Thankfully, it was the last time that Leeds has been in fear of attack though many servicemen from the Leeds area have been involved in conflict since, notably in recent years in the Falkland and the war to liberate Iraq.

12 SPORT

Sports before Victorian times almost invariably had an animal cruelty element to them. Cockfighting, of which there were several rings in the city, and bull baiting were largely working class pursuits; the area still known as the Bull Ring in Lower Wortley was still organising baiting as recently as the 1820s.

Cock-fighting regularly took place at the *Talbot Inn* and, though popular among the working classes, it was condemned by many. People wrote to the papers of the time, the *Leeds Mercury* and the *Intelligencer* arguing for an end to 'this barbarous sport held for no other purpose than to give an opportunity of making bets.' In August 1725, as a forerunner to the races, a main of cocks took place at Chapeltown with stakes reaching as high as a hundred guineas.

Cockfighting, in its early days was mainly an inter-county affair or a contest between a town or parish against another. An advert in 1742 captures this, pitting the men of Yorkshire against their counterparts from Lancashire. Another advert advertises a contest between the gentlemen of Leeds and those from Knaresborough in a bout to be held, once again, at the *Talbot Inn*.

Woodhouse Moor, scene of early sporting activity. The author

The lower classes were increasingly attracted to brutal spectacles and bare fist fighting was another popular pursuit with many people flocking to see such an event, often at Woodhouse Moor where there were boxing booths set up.

Woodhouse Moor was also the scene for cockfights where the spectacle used to take several hours and large crowds assembled. It was a common sight to see the cocks drinking the ale out of their owner's pint glasses in the public houses where they lodged for the night. Dog fighting and pigeon shooting were other cruel sports for the masses, though in the case of pigeon shooting it could also be hazardous to the human race as more than one person was killed through indulging in this activity.

Horses and ponies, belonging to local farmers and gentry, were allowed to run loose on the Moor and where the almshouses in St Mark's Road are now situated was a small lake and some plantation where the horses could parade and exercise.

It had been an offence to ride a horse on the Moor but this was abolished and people were often seen there riding on horseback. Indeed, horse racing was held there in the mid-nineteenth century, though the practice ended soon after a jockey was killed in a fall. There was also a Leeds Hunt and the dogs were kept in kennels in a row of cottages near the Belle Vue entrance to the main moor, thought to be called Sportsmans Row. The Leeds Hunt first took place about 1740 and by the end of the century, it was meeting about three times a week.

During the 1700s the Leeds Races were an integral part of the social calendar. The *Talbot Inn*, as well as a haven for cockfighting, was also used as a venue for weighing the horses before they were rode out onto Chapeltown Moor.

The Leeds Races were resurrected between 1824 and 1830 when it was held at Haigh Park near the River Aire, attracting crowds of around 50,000, especially for the main Golden Tureen Race. The racecourse did not attract clientele solely from the working classes, as middle classes, though they often frowned at the sport, were only too eager to participate in the gambling which invariably surrounded the race.

Other sport in Leeds in the middle of the eighteenth century saw a race between footmen. These were men who accompanied carriages on foot and helped them with the aid of a pole to lift the vehicles out of ruts in the road. The men were often called running footmen as they had to have the ability to run or jog.

An advert appeared in 1741:

To be run for on Chappeltown Moor near Leedes on Monday March 24th, three pounds by footmen twice round the usual course to be entered at Widow Knubley's at the Crown in Upperhead-Row, Leedes.

Chapeltown Moor was also a popular venue for others interested in athletics or 'foot races' as they were known.

Other people in Leeds chose archery. An Act of Parliament of 1541 established that every able-bodied man in the country had to be able to use a long bow and special areas were created so that men could practice their archery. One such area, Butts Court, survives to the present day.

During the mid-1800s there was an archery ground in Blackman Lane, adjoining Blenheim Square and here, in spring and summer, the members of the Leeds Archery Society, formed in 1848, practised their skills resplendent in dark green uniforms.

In 1866 there was an organisation called the Leeds Ladies Archery Society, which had an annual field day, whilst those interested in shooting could join the Leeds Rifles Society with shooting taking place at the Middleton range.

The council had provided six swimming pools in the city by the end of the nineteenth century and there was also an increase in the provision of park area and recreation grounds. Woodhouse Moor and Bramley were already established before 1870, but in 1871 the situation improved considerably when the Nicholson Estate towards the north of the town was purchased for £127,000. The public were slow to realise what an asset they had in the new Roundhay Park, believing it to be a waste of money as it was too far away for most of the population who still lived in a concentrated area in inner Leeds. However, a tram route was built to link the park with the town and it soon became a popular retreat for the people of Leeds.

In the late 1800s private enterprise complemented the council's provisions ensuring that public recreation took a step forward. The Royal Park to the west of Woodhouse Moor was the most popular commercial open space in Leeds at the time. However, by 1875 half of the space had been sold for housing whilst the other half was sold to the Leeds Horticultural Gardens Company which used the space for an indoor skating rink, a bowling green, a gym, a cricket pitch and lawns. However, this imaginative use of leisure facilities itself failed and was sold in 1884.

Organised sport enjoyed a surge in popularity in the nineteenth century and in March 1864, an advert appeared in the *Leeds Mercury* calling for men interested in football to form a team to play on Woodhouse Moor. The Football Association had been founded a year earlier and the rules of the game were quickly becoming established.

Football took quite some time before becoming established in Leeds, as during the Victorian era, rugby was dominant during the winter months. Early attempts to introduce the Leeds public to football were not a great success, greeted as they were largely by indifference.

The situation was different in Sheffield where rugby was not as popular. The oldest football club in the world was formed in Sheffield in 1857 and the game was transported to other parts of Yorkshire with the first match to take place in Leeds being organised by football pioneers from Sheffield. It was arranged by Fred Sanderson, President of the Sheffield Football Association who brought over two teams to play in an exhibition match at Holbeck Recreation Ground on Boxing Day 1877.

Despite a biting cold wind the game managed to attract a big crowd, though it later emerged that many of the spectators were season-ticket holders at Holbeck Rugby club who had been able to get into the ground for free! Though the centre of Leeds was largely a football-free zone during Victorian times, there was more interest on the outskirts of the town with both Rothwell and Oulton having teams.

In 1881 Rothwell fixed up a match with Blackburn Rovers, again played at the Holbeck ground, though once again it failed to generate much interest amongst the Leeds public. However, as the rest of the country slowly became attracted to the game, interest in football in Leeds grew and the first club in the city was formed by Leonard Cooper at Kirkstall in 1885, simply called Leeds.

The first match for Leeds was against Hull Town at Armley Cricket Ground in Armley Park on 3 October 1885. However, as appeared to be quite a common occurrence in those early days of football, the opposition failed to turn up!

This club soon folded but two new clubs had emerged by 1888, Leeds and Leeds Albion with Leeds playing at Kirkstall and Albion at Brudenell Road. In 1894 the West Yorkshire League was formed.

However, even though football was now becoming an established winter sport throughout the country, it was still struggling to find its feet in West Yorkshire, largely due to the predominance of rugby.

By 1891 these two clubs had failed and organised football matches had largely vanished from Leeds, but help was on hand coincidentally thanks to rugby! There was a dispute in rugby through which rugby League was formed. However, for a time the two codes of rugby fought for domination and while rugby was out of action football was able to take advantage of the desire for spectator sport which had already taken hold.

Football organisers in the city, eager to press home this advantage, realised that spectators were keen to see games which had more of a competitive edge to them as opposed to the 'exhibition matches' they had previously been force-fed on and leagues were formed as were cup competitions which helped to give most games some interest to spectators.

At the turn of the century Hunslet football club was the main team in the city and they played in the first football game at Elland Road, against Harrogate on 23 April 1898. Elland Road was a turnpike road opened in 1785 and later became the site of the Leeds Greyhound Stadium which was opened in 1927. However, from the early twentieth century it became known for being the main football venue in the city.

Leeds City football club was formed following the closure of the Hunslet club and took over its Elland Road lease, building the West Stand at the ground. By November 1904 the new club was ready to play competitive football and the first match took place, at Elland Road versus Hull City. The 3,000 crowd was entertained by a local boy's match and a band and the stage was set for the main event, but Leeds disappointed the supporters by losing the match 2–0.

Elland Road as it looks today. The author

Leeds City were elected to the Football League with the first match taking place on 2 September 1905. However, within a few years the club had been thrown out of the league for making illegal payments to players. Leeds United was formed and took over at Elland Road before being elected to the Midland League on 31 October 1913. In 1920 the club was elected back to the Football League and eventually won promotion to the First Division.

Rugby, however, established itself far quicker as a popular sport in the town. By the 1880s, most churches ran their own rugby club as it was seen as a healthy way of enticing men away from the traditional leisure pursuits of drinking and gambling.

Rugby League has its origins in a famous meeting at the George Hotel in Huddersfield in August 1895, though even before this date there was activity in Leeds. In 1870 a Leeds St John's team began playing fixtures, most of which took place at the Cardigan Fields. The club grew in stature and made a Yorkshire Cup Final appearance in 1887.

Leeds St John became the football section of the Leeds Cricket, Football and Athletics Company Ltd. Under their new name the club

Headingley at the turn of the century. The author

fulfilled some more games at Cardigan Fields before moving to Headingley, the new headquarters of the Leeds sporting company.

The opening match at their new ground was against Manningham on 20 September 1890. Most of the union clubs had players who were forced to work on Saturdays and they were subsequently torn between work and play. To play for their union clubs meant taking time off work and the resultant loss of wages. Some clubs paid compensation to these players but the Rugby Union strongly disapproved of this, leading to a revolt amongst the players and clubs.

Campaigning began and the final split in rugby came on 29 August 1895 when the leading clubs of Lancashire and Yorkshire met to form their own union which eventually became known as rugby league.

League became a popular sport in Yorkshire and Lancashire and Leeds was host to three professional teams, Leeds, Hunslet and Bramley. Headingley is still home to Leeds Rugby League with the team now known as the Leeds Rhinos, however rugby union is also based at the famous old ground with the Leeds Tykes playing their home games here.

Most cricket games during the eighteenth century were played for a stake and betting was rife amongst followers of the game. In one early game in 1766 the married men of Leeds played the

Hunslet rugby team of 1889. Hunslet Rugby Club

bachelors of the town for a bet of five guineas plus dinner. The bachelors won by six wickets. In the 1820s most cricket matches played in Leeds were double-innings affairs with run aggregates often less than 200.

The first recorded three-day cricket match in Leeds took place on Woodhouse Moor in 1846 when the All-England XI beat eighteen of Yorkshire by sixty-nine runs. Very few matches took place at this time with midweek fixtures being more common than weekend games; evidence that the games popularity at this time was limited mainly to the gentry.

Cricket developed in popularity between 1850 and 1880 due to the railway boom providing passenger services to the towns of the West Riding. Also, the 1850 Factories Act ensured a five and a half-day working week for the majority of the workforce. This meant that more cricketers, including those from the middle and lower classes, had time to play the game, especially at weekends. It was also easier for players and spectators to travel to games due to the new transport system in operation. Therefore, watching sport, as well as playing it, became something of an accepted recreational activity on a Saturday afternoon.

In 1888 plans were formulated to provide Leeds with a sporting venue, something which, by now was needed. The Leeds Cricket, Football and Athletics Company was formed and the world famous Headingley was a step nearer becoming reality. For some time the Headingley ground was the sole centre for organised sport in the area. Cricket and Rugby Union were played there, as is the case today. However, when the ground first opened, it was also a stage for lawn tennis, bowls, athletics and cycling. Football was also played there for a short time.

The first cricket match at Headingley was between Leeds and Scarborough on 27 May 1890 in front of a crowd of 5,000. The *Yorkshire Post* reported the event saying:

> *The newly laid out ground of Leeds cricket, football and athletic company at Headingley was informally opened on Tuesday, 27 May when a match between Leeds and Scarborough cricket clubs took place. The crowd increased as the day wore on and the final figure was estimated at about 5,000.*

The crease was described as being in first rate condition and the facilities for the spectators were also very good with the Grand Pavilion in particular, being an elegant structure. A considerable

Headingley in more recent times. The author

amount of work had been done at the ground to make it suitable for cricket, football, tennis and athletics. The paper added that if work continued at the venue to the same high standard, it would be the most complete centre of athletic competition in the north of England.

The first county game was a year later in June 1891 when Yorkshire entertained Derbyshire and the ground first played host to a Test match on 29 June 1899 when England took on Australia for the Ashes. England lost that game and had to wait until 1907 for their first win in Leeds. That came in June 1907 when they beat South Africa by fifty-three runs with Colin Blythe taking 15–99.

The Headingley test matches became an institution amongst the cricket going public with it being a focal point for test cricket in the north, something which continues to this day. It was also a day for socialising, eating and drinking whilst watching leather doing battle with willow. During the Ashes test match at Headingley in 1905 between England and Australia, which was won by the Aussies, over 54,000 attended the match over the three days and the *Yorkshire Evening Post* took a particular interest in exactly how much food and drink was consumed by those at the ground. It reported that several hundred baskets of strawberries were eaten at Headingley during the three days while the local representatives of the banana shippers estimate that the test match made a difference in their ordinary sale of 450 bunches.

It was estimated that about 64,000 bananas were eaten with a large proportion of these being sold by hawkers outside the enclosure. About 10,000 pork pies were also sold and at least 50,000 bottles of beer were drunk as well as several thousand glasses of whisky and scores of gallons of mineral water as well as tea.

Headingley has seen many cricketing highlights since its inception as a test match venue. Australia's all-time world averages leader Sir Donald Bradman scored triple centuries at Headingley in 1930 and 1934 and it was also the scene of possibly England's best come-from-behind victory when Ian Botham engineered a rear-guard effort in 1981 to beat Australia by 18 runs after being forced to follow-on.

By the twentieth century organised sporting events were growing in popularity. Cricket, football and rugby were largely played at the weekend and were an ever-popular retreat, mainly for the working man.

Football, rugby and cricket were the main spectator sports in Leeds but there were other pastimes and by the twentieth century, many employers began to organise social and sporting events for their

The recently refurbished Headingley. The author

York Road Baths. The author

employees. Burtons was a prime example and was noted for its billiards and tennis club.

More public baths opened in the city and the York Road baths opened in Leeds in 1905 as the newly acquired passion for leisure time gathered pace. A report at the time highlighted the York Road 'Russian Bath' which was of, 'special design and construction and consists of a suite of three rooms; hot room, shower room and cooling room. The hot room has fittings for obtaining any steam heat required.'

New schools, including the West Leeds High School which opened in Armley in the early part of the twentieth century, were keen to highlight the importance of recreation to children. The new school had football, cricket and hockey pitches with tennis and croquet lawns. Roller skating was popular in schools for a time as was football which was often played with a cricket ball to quite primitive rules. There was also competition between spinning tops and some schools had gym facilities with some children excelling at the horizontal and parallel bars.

Golf also took off as a sport to participate in. Moortown golf club was founded in 1909 with its course designed by Dr Alistair Mackenzie. An exhibition match between the Open champion, James Braid and the legendary Harry Vardon marked the opening of the course. The present clubhouse was opened in 1915 and in 1929 the club was host to the first Ryder Cup match to be played on British soil.

Moortown Golf Club, scene of the first Ryder Cup held on British soil. The author

In the twenty-first century, Leeds is still highly regarded in sporting circles. Leeds United still play at Elland Road and Headingley cricket ground has undergone extensive redevelopment in recent years. On the other side of the main stand still sits Headingley rugby ground with both codes of rugby now played here.

Select Bibliography

A Leeds Loiner, H Sydney Pickering (Abbey Press, 1985)

A History of Leeds, WR Mitchell (Phillimore & Co, 2000)

Autobiography, Israel Roberts (Wesley Historical Society, 1984)

Blue Plaques of Leeds, Peter Dyson and Kevin Grady (Leeds Civic Trust, 2001)

Dean Hook, C J Stranks (A R Mowbray & Co Ltd, 1954)

Images of Leeds 1850–1960, Peter Brears (Breedon Books, 1989)

Leeds A to Z of local history, John Gilleghan MBE (Kingsway Press, 2001)

Leeds, Ivan Broadhead (Smith Settle Publishing, 1990)

Leeds: The heart of Yorkshire, John Waddington-Feather (Amethyst Press, 1984)

Leeds Pals, Laurie Milner (Leo Cooper, 1991)

Leeds: The story of a city, David Thornton (Fort Publishing, 2002)

Leeds Transport, J Soper (Leeds Transport Historical Society, 1985)

The Canal & River Sections of the Air and Calder Navigation, Mike Taylor (Wharncliffe Books, 2003)

The Illustrated History of Leeds, Steven Burt and Kevin Grady (Breedon Books, 2002)

The Leeds Rugby League Story, Dave Callaghan (Breedon Books, 1992)

To prove I'm not forgot, Sylvia M Barnard (Manchester University Press, 1990)

INDEX